Brigid's Mantle

*A Celtic Dialogue
Between Pagan and Christian*

Brigid's Mantle

A Celtic Dialogue Between Pagan and Christian

LILLY WEICHBERGER & KENNETH MCINTOSH

ANAMCHARA
BOOKS

Brigid's Mantle:
A Celtic Dialogue Between Pagan and Christian

Copyright © 2015 by Anamchara Books, a division of Harding House Publishing Service, Inc. All rights reserved. No part of this publication may be reproduced or transmitted in any form or by any means, electronic or mechanical, including photocopying, recording, taping, or any information storage and retrieval system, without permission from the publisher.

Anamchara Books
Vestal, NY 13850
www.anamcharabooks.com

Ingram Spark 2020 paperback ISBN: 978-1-62524-811-4

Author: Lilly Weichberger & Kenneth McIntosh.
Cover design by Ellyn Sanna.
Interior design by Camden Flath.

The scripture quotation labeled NLT is taken from the Holy Bible, New Living Translation, copyright ©1996, 2004, 2007. Used by permission of Tyndale House Publishers, Inc., Carol Stream, Illinois 60188. All rights reserved. The scripture quotation labeled NASB is taken from the New American Standard Bible®, copyright © 1960, 1962, 1963, 1968, 1971, 1972, 1973, 1975, 1977, 1995 by The Lockman Foundation. Used by permission. (www.Lockman.org).

Hail, Brigid! Keeper of the forge,
she who shapes the world itself with fire,
she who ignites the spark of passion in the poets,
she who leads the clans with a warrior's cry,
she who is the bride of the islands,
and who leads the fight of freedom.
Hail, Brigid! Defender of kin and hearth,
she who inspires the bards to sing,
she who drives the smith to raise his hammer,
she who is a fire sweeping across the land.
—Clann Bhride, Book of Hours

*Spread thy mantle, O Brigid,
Mary of the Gael.
May thy protection never fail.
Spread thy mantle over me,
where'er I pass, where'er I be.
Weather foul or weather fair,
keep me in thy loving care.
Till I rest, my journeys o'er,
with God and thee forevermore.*
—Rita Minehan

A Note to the Reader from the Authors

First of all, we want to tell you who we are:

Lilly Weichberger is a healer, teacher, and eternal student of the Celtic Shamanic tradition. In the pursuit of deepening connection with the Divine, she works with students of many backgrounds, both individually and through group classes and workshops, both locally and across the country, to help individuals find and strengthen their power and their own unique connections to the Earth and to the Infinite. Her teaching focuses on a synthesis of Shamanism, Magic, and Celtic spirituality to help bring individuals into a more direct and personal relationship with the Divine, in whatever form is most appropriate to them. She was raised on the East Coast, but after traveling extensively and moving frequently (including time spent living and studying Shamanism, Druidry, and Sorcery in the UK), she has recently settled in Oregon, where she pursues a variety of interests, in addition to her healing, writing, and teaching work. She is currently completing her degree in Viticulture and Enology, and she has launched Mabinogion Meadery in tandem with a Welsh company.

Kenneth McIntosh is a writer, educator, and spiritual mentor. As a child he became fascinated with the Celtic legends of his heritage, and then as a young adult he experienced a profound spiritual conversion that led to him becoming a follower of Jesus of Nazareth. Degrees in English and theology, combined with travels in the Middle East and the Celtic lands of Ireland, Scotland, and Wales, further inspired his life and writing. He is best known for his book *Water from an Ancient Well: Celtic Spirituality for Modern Life*, but he has also recently authored a young adult fantasy titled *Magic Reversed*, which is set in Celtic lands during the Dark Ages. The novel is part of a trilogy, and the sequel will be published soon. In addition to writing, he teaches comparative religions at a community college and serves as pastor for a Congregational Church.

This book started out as an actual spoken dialogue between us. Since then, we've expanded our thoughts into book form. Some sections were written by both of us together; most sections were written by one or the other. We've indicated which one of us is speaking throughout. A few brief sections were added by our editor at Anamchara Books.

The woman we've focused on in our dialogue has numerous names, with various pronunciations and spellings. For this book we've chosen the spelling "Brigid," which in Irish Gaelic is pronounced the same as if it were spelled "Brigit." Our choice of spelling is not intended to favor one particular tradition over another: the variety of spellings and pronunciations of her name do not change the meaning of who she is!

1
Celtic Spirituality: An Overview

Thanks to her roles as both a Pagan Goddess and a Christian saint, Brigid is often seen as a vital connection between the old Pagan ways and the newer ways of those who followed the teachings of Jesus. Her mantle covers both perspectives.

According to legend, when the Christian Brigid went to the king of Leinster to ask for land so she could build an abbey, the king flippantly told her he'd be happy to give her as much land as she could cover with her mantle. To his astonishment, Brigid's mantle grew and grew until it covered the wide piece of land she needed. Meanwhile, in Pagan stories, Brigid's mantle carried within it blessings and powers of healing; to place friends and loved ones "under Brigid's mantle" was to invoke protection and renewal for them.

As you read this book, think of Brigid's mantle as Celtic spirituality, a term that's wide enough to cover many perspectives beneath its shelter, even while it means different things to different people. For some it's an ancient form of Christianity, one that's particularly appealing to modern followers of Jesus who want a faith that focuses on justice, tolerance, equality for women, creativity, and a love of Nature. For others, Celtic spirituality is a way to connect with a pre-Christian perspective on the world, one that celebrates the Earth and her seasons, finding deep spiritual meaning in land and sea and air. Celtic spirituality offers a place of commonality between the two.

A mantle is not rigid. It's not a box that keeps some things in and others out. Instead, its cloth is wide, sheltering, inclusive. Within Brigid's mantle, both Christian and Pagan can find the Divine presence revealed in the ordinary patterns of daily life. They can draw close to the Divine in outdoor places, and they can look to the past to find new patterns of life for the twenty-first century. Perhaps most of all, within the folds of Celtic spirituality we find a world that's lit with wonder.

Kenneth

To talk intelligently about Brigid and her role in Celtic spirituality, we need to understand what we mean by the word "Celtic." Today, the word is sometimes equated with all things old and legendary, with dungeons-and-dragons magic and Renaissance-faire make-believe—and with beautiful spiral patterns that make really amazing tattoos! But the Celts were a living, breathing reality. So before we focus on Celtic spiritually, let's set the historical and cultural context from which it grew.

The Celts were a large and diverse group of people that came out of Eastern Europe five centuries or so before the time of Christ. Their commonality was found in certain broad patterns of language, culture, and genetics. The ancient Greeks make first mention of them, calling them *Keltoi* and describing them as "proud, boastful, and high spirited." (This still describes most of us Celts-in-diaspora today!) The ancient Celts had a fearless sense of *carpe diem*: seize the day. "Don't sit home and be bored," they would have advised you. "Go out there and explore. Life is beautiful—and limitless!"

For the Celts (both Pagan and Christian), the creation of beautiful things in every medium—music, visual art, metalwork, architecture, sculpture, poem, and story—was an essential part of experiencing life. Archaeologists have found incredible metalwork in pre-Christian Iron Age sites in LaTene, Switzerland; Hallstatt, Austria; and elsewhere. The Christian Celts of the Dark Ages created amazing books illuminated with intertwining patterns and jewel-toned animals. They were poets and storytellers who passed down to their descendents a rich written and spoken tradition.

Today, the Celts often seem as though they inhabited a misty, magic world alongside woodland elves and sprites, but historically, they were also a formidable military force. In 390 BCE, a Gallic (Celtic) tribe faced a Roman army twice its size, conquered them, and went on to sack Rome. In a time span of only a few centuries, the Celtic tribes, with their combination of bravery, mysticism, and craftsmanship, conquered most of modern Europe.

The Celtic peoples likely share a common ancestry with the modern-day inhabitants of India, which explains the close connections between Celtic-Druidic traditions and Hindu mythology, spirituality, and culture. Even today, there are more than two hundred words that are almost identical between Gaelic and Sanskrit, including *brihati*—"exalted one," "light bringer," or "bright one"—the root word for Brigid's name. Archaeologists have also found mummies from the early Iron Age in Xinjiang, China, with Celtic red hair, physical features, clothing, and artwork. That's how far the Celts spread in their early years!

The seesaw reality of war and conquest shapes the history of nearly all groups of people, and the Celts' history has had its share. Starting in 50 BCE, the Celtic tribes that had once swept victorious from Asia to Europe faced Julius Caesar's vast and ferocious campaign. The outcome was by no means inevitable, and battles were closely pitched. In the end, however, the Latin Empire swallowed up Celtic lands throughout Europe and even into Britain; only the Picts (in modern-day Scotland) and the Irish remained unvanquished.

During the time that Rome was growing to its greatest size, an impoverished Jewish couple gave birth to a peasant boy in a barn in Roman-occupied Judea. After that boy reached adulthood, the Romans killed him; doubtless for them, the act was as banal as the killing of cattle and swine to supply the legions' larders. But the followers of this Jewish man insisted that he wasn't really dead, and that teaching spread underground so powerfully that three centuries later, a majority of Roman citizens worshiped the Nail-Riven One as their God. So it was inevitable that Christ worship eventually made its way to the Celtic lands. Historians can't say when the gospel first came to the Gaels, but legends fill in the blank pages of history.

There's a story—first written down many centuries after it was said to have happened—that Joseph of Arimathea, the rich Jewish man who donated the tomb where Jesus was buried, fled from the anger of his people's ruling council. Joseph was a tin merchant with ships that sailed to southern Britain collecting precious ore from the mines there, so with Mary Magdalene and some other friends, he set sail for what is now Great Britain.

Other legends say that Joseph of Arimathea was a friend of Joseph and Mary who had taken the young Jesus with him on one of his merchant trips to Britain. Based on that old story, William Blake wrote these famous lines:

> *And did those feet in ancient time*
> *Walk upon England's mountains green?*
> *And was the holy Lamb of God*
> *On England's pleasant pastures seen?*

According to these legends, Joseph of Arimathea eventually established the first Christian church in Britain at Glastonbury, and its peculiar treasure would be the Holy Grail. Of course there's no way to prove this mythical account as historical; nonetheless *someone* established a very early church in the Glastonbury area during the time when the Britons—a Celtic tribal group—lived there.

There are several other instances of Gallic people receiving the Jesus message before the dawning of the Golden Age of Celtic Christianity. An early Celtic theologian was Morgan of Wales, better known by his Latin name of Pelagius. Like most Celts, he held the virtue of human freedom in great esteem, and his championship of free will in theological circles got him condemned by the far more famous theologian Augustine. To this day, some Christians equate "Pelagian" with the ugly word "heretic"—and yet this Welshman was a scrupulous scholar of the Bible and famous for his disciplined-yet-compassionate life. Though condemned by the Western bishops, Celtic believers never repudiated him. Saint Martin of Tours is another famous Celtic Christian from the time of the Roman Empire. He developed a way of life that was the most important monastic model until Benedict of Nursia's monasticism became standardized.

What people today think of as Celtic Christianity, however, is most associated with one enormously influential man. Maywen Succat—better known by his Latin name Patrick—was born to a Romanized Welsh family just at the time when Rome pulled its legions out of Britain. With the Romans gone, the British coast became easy pickings for Irish slavers, and on one of their raids, they snatched up teenage Patrick. He was sold to a chieftain in the northwest of Ireland and slaved there for six awful years before a miraculous voice from heaven told him how to escape. As a fugitive, he ran clear across Ireland, found the ship that had been prophesied to him, and sailed back to his home. And then the real miracle happened.

God spoke to Patrick in a dream, urging him back to the land of his enslavement in order to spread the gospel, even though as an escaped slave he would face the threat of death. He did return—and by the end of his life he had converted at least the northern portion of Ireland. This is where our heroine Brigid comes into the Christian version of her story. She came to follow Jesus at the start of her teen years, while Patrick was still walking around the island telling stories of the Christ.

Brigid became one of the powerful symbolic bridges that enabled many of the ancient Irish to cross over into following Christ. Somehow, the ancient Pagan Goddess and a Christian saint merged into one woman. In Heather Terrell's novel version of the story, *Brigid of Kildare*, she offers what seems to me to be a plausible explanation for why this happened. In the novel, Brigid struggles on two fronts for the soul of Ireland: she longs to introduce her people to Christ, yet she also faces threats from Imperial Rome's Christianity, which was disempowering women in the church. Brigid strikes upon a brilliant strategy that accomplishes both her aims at the same time; she deliberately takes upon herself the persona of her namesake, the Goddess. She dresses and acts in ways that invoke her people's mythic understanding of Brigid. Doing so, she gains esteem for her Christian message and at the same time affirms traditional Irish views of women's equality. We can't know if this was actually the case, but it would explain how Brigid of the Sidhe and Brigid the historical Christian spokeswoman became one. However it happened, the Christian Brigid was a brilliant and dynamic leader whose faith owed much to Patrick's legacy.

Patrick was a genius in the art of communication. Although he lived at the time when Christianity was beginning to look very much like the Roman Empire—globalized, standardized, and spread by means of force—he followed the earlier ways of the homegrown Jesus movement. He spread his religious message by attraction rather than compulsion, singing songs (the Irish always love that), telling stories (they love that also), and living as a poor wanderer without a sword to defend himself (*that* must have amazed them).

It can be tricky separating the historical Patrick from the legends that grew around him, but judging from the fruits of his labors, we can surmise that Patrick intentionally looked for elements of Christianity and Paganism that ran parallel to one another. These were not hard to find in Celtic culture. While the Druids are commonly portrayed (outside Pagan circles) as human-sacrificing priests, these "oak-knowers" (the literal meaning of the word *druid*) held the respect of the Pagan Irish for very good reasons. Unlike other cultures, if the Irish did sacrifice mortal blood, the victims volunteered to participate in a lottery from among their own ranks—so Druid sacrifice, Patrick pointed out, was similar to the crucifixion of Jesus, who chose to die for others. The Druids wore unbleached garments to signify their commonality with the poorer classes, and Patrick's priests intentionally did the same. The Druids baptized children at birth in holy wells, and it seems likely that Patrick followed that practice, substituting "Father, Son, and Spirit" for the names of the threefold Irish Deities.

One thing that Christianity brought to the Celts was a written language. The Druids had themselves been living treasure-houses of wisdom, wisdom that had been passed along orally for centuries, but now everyone who could read had access to all manner of knowledge. With their love of creativity and the arts, the Celts quickly embraced the written art form, beginning a passionate love affair that has never died.

What's more, they didn't practice censorship. They believed in preserving all traditions of humankind. These early Celtic Christians even sought out Druids and said, "We don't want the old traditions to become lost. Tell us your legends." They recorded ancient Celtic tales—where heroes were constantly lopping off heads—with as much faithfulness as they did the Bible and other Christian writings. If Celtic Christian monks had not written down these oral traditions, many of the pre-Christian legends and sagas would have disappeared into the mists of time. Christian monks saved these stories so that the world did not forget them. They wrote down all manner of things—and they also made writing into an art form.

During two weeks in Ireland recently, only once did I have to wait in a queue (a line). Early in the morning on a weekday in Dublin, hundreds of people stood waiting patiently for forty-five minutes or more. We weren't waiting for a ride at Disneyland; we were waiting to see the Book of Kells, a gorgeous, eighth-century Irish manuscript that proves the way Celtic Christians transformed the written word into amazing, utterly beautiful designs and patterns.

In a book titled *How the Irish Saved Civilization*, historian Thomas Cahill makes the point that the world has overlooked its deep debt to the Celts. When the Roman Empire collapsed beneath the onslaught of the Huns and Germanic tribes, many of Europe's centers of learning and reading were destroyed. Meanwhile, though, safe on their misty green island, Irish monks were preserving the ancient world's legacy of knowledge and wisdom, patiently copying countless texts. In many cases, these would be the only copies to survive the Dark Ages. Today we are still learning from them.

Lilly

The Celts have always treasured learning. It's a common strand that has never been lost in Celtic culture. In the pre-Christian Celtic world, where each *tuath*—tribe or clan—had its own chieftain and its own Deities, as well as tribal connections and alliances based on a complicated system of blood ties and loyalties, the Druids, the keepers of knowledge, were the glue that bound the Celts together into a coherent, ongoing whole. The Druids maintained a vast storehouse of knowledge, both spiritual and mundane, that endured for centuries.

Their wisdom was never written down; to do so was considered taboo. Instead, as part of the long process of becoming a Druid, a person had to spend twenty years memorizing lineages, laws, herbal knowledge, and history. The Druids' immense collection of knowledge was stored entirely within human brains, and it was passed from generation to generation entirely through the memorization of verbal teaching.

The Celts are often nearly fanatical about the things they love. A Scottish friend of mine once joked, "We Celts don't do anything by half measures. We live passionately, love passionately, hate passionately, and die passionately." The Celts were outstanding artists and scholars, warriors and saints. Most of all, they were—and they still are—adventurers who dared leave the familiar and explore new places, both physically and spiritually.

The Celts have also always loved good music, art, and food. (At least we can say they loved to eat, even if some people have joked that their traditional foods were less of a cuisine and more of a penance!) They treasured good company, and the bonds of kinship were vitally important to them. Celts might fight like cats and dogs within the family, but anyone who threatened the clan would find himself facing a solid wall of opposition.

Most of all, the Celts loved the Divine presence they found everywhere they turned. It wasn't separate from ordinary life. It wasn't "out there" somewhere; it was here, now. As I've come to know Kenneth, I've found that same awareness of the Divine, a strong, deep thread that crosses back and forth between our two traditions. Because of that thread, I can't help but find myself nodding and nodding as I listen to what Kenneth has to say.

Kenneth

I too find myself nodding in agreement with Lilly. We share many common understandings. But I want to expand on that statement with a few words of further explanation. Brigid's mantle is wide enough to encompass differences—but it doesn't take away the reality of those differences. The assumption that "all religions (or all spiritualities) are really the same" is a simplistic one. Lilly and I are not saying that beneath their external differences, Paganism and Christianity are actually the same thing. Both our traditions have distinctive strengths that we each value and hold on to.

Within Brigid's mantle we find a bridge between our traditions; in fact, we have come to discover a good number of such bridges. But the existence of a bridge between two things does not mean they are identical. If they were, there would be no need for a bridge! The bridges Lilly and I have found beneath Brigid's mantle enrich our lives. They give us new perspectives on our own beliefs, and they teach us new ways to deepen our faith. But we do not use those bridges to try to either convert the other or erase the real differences between us.

I've thought about the topic of interfaith dialogue a good deal, since I've taught comparative religions at the college level for a number of years. The very nature of a class titled "Comparative Religions" proves that the religions of the world do have many points of comparison. As students delve deeper into each tradition, they are able to point out more and more points of commonality. At the same time, if they are comprehending the concepts, students also discover an increasing number of points where the religions differ from one another, where each is unique.

So the discussion within this book is not an attempt to minimize distinctions between Christianity and the Old Religion. It is a *dialogue*. It differs from a debate because it is cordial and collegial; Lilly and I are friends, we share a mutual respect for each other, and neither of us is attempting to convert the other. We discuss a variety of topics—centered on a figure common to both our faiths—in order to explore where we share common understandings and where we differ.

While I'm at it, this seems like a good place to address another misunderstanding I sometimes hear: well-intentioned but poorly informed fellow believers in Christ often criticize Celtic Christianity as being influenced by Paganism. I don't deny that many factors of the ancient Celtic cultural milieu helped shape Celtic Christian beliefs and practices. I don't see that as a bad thing.

All forms of Christianity over the past two millennia have been influenced by their surrounding cultures. The early Church Fathers in the West filled copious pages writing about both the similarities and distinctions between Christianity and Greco-Roman philosophy. Eastern Christians were influenced by their pre-Christian cultural assumptions derived from Middle Eastern traditions, while after the fourth century, Western Christianity was largely shaped by the philosophies of the crumbling Roman Empire. In the Middle Ages, the influence of Platonic and Aristotelian philosophy on Western Christianity became more pronounced, and the assumptions of the feudal European class system also molded major Christian doctrines. New philosophical concepts during the Renaissance and Enlightenment were what triggered the Protestant Reformation. Today, even the most conservative forms of contemporary Christian theology are expressed entirely within the assumptions of modernity. However much modern-day fundamentalists may condemn science, they too have bought into its largest ideas, such as gravity, the solar system, and the existence of outer space. No Christians today would say, "The Earth is flat and immovable; the sun revolves around the Earth"—and yet when Galileo's radical theories were first presented, many Christians resisted belief in them for fear they contradicted the Bible.

So yes, Celtic Christianity was influenced by its surrounding cultural context, just as all forms of religious belief are shaped by their cultural milieus. No one can honestly claim, "My religion is free from cultural contamination." God has always communicated within the contexts of human cultures, languages, and traditions. Any genuine spirituality must be *embodied*, and therefore every expression of faith comes within the larger milieu of its surrounding ideas, norms, and assumptions. Every expression of spiritual faith—whether Christian or Pagan, Muslim or Hindu, Jewish or Buddhist—is flavored by cultural factors. I respect believers in any religion who concede the inevitability of enculturation and attempt to understand what that means within their own faiths. This is one of my goals in my dialogue with Lilly, in this book.

One of the cultural factors that the Celts brought to Christianity was their love of the number three. They saw the world in terms of sacred threes: earth, sea, and sky; the Underworld, the Earth, Heaven; the unity of time in past, present, and future. Anything the Celts repeated three times was given extra power, and their poetry often took the form of three-line stanzas. So when they were introduced to a religion that said God is "Three-in-One and One-in-Three," it made perfect sense to them.

Other Christian traditions became fixated on singular aspects of the Deity, hence there are "Jesus only" Christians, and there are also some Pentecostal traditions that focus more exclusively on the Holy Spirit. Some recent theologians speak of succeeding Christian eras—that of the Father, then the Son, and now the Spirit. The early Celtic Christian tradition, however, did not focus on a single aspect of the Divine. Their perspective was balanced and in harmony, allowing them to invoke and worship equally all three aspects of the Godhead. They felt no need for long philosophical discussions about the Trinity. It seemed perfectly natural to them to think of God as being threefold: Maker, Redeemer, and Sustainer, one in being. My father was a Unitarian who put no stock in the Trinity, but as a Celtic Christian, I have come to appreciate the sense of balance and wholeness found in relating to a threefold God.

Another thing that the Celtic Christian tradition teaches me is to put very little stock in inflexible traditions. I have learned to have a flexible perspective on spirituality, rather than insisting that my personal beliefs are the only correct ones. Each person will interact with the Divine in a unique way (and yes, it will be shaped by culture, as well as family background and individual personalities). The Celts understood this.

After Christianity took root in the soil of the ancient, indigenous Celtic traditions, many people—Patrick, Brigid, and others—brought the epic tales of the Bible and Gospels to various groups of Celts. For centuries, entire communities were asking, "How does the story of Christ combine with the story of my people? What does it mean to be truly Welsh and a follower of Jesus? What does it mean to be truly Irish while traveling the Jesus path?" The planting of the gospel seed in the differing soils of Celtic lands produced many varieties of fruit!

This means that Celtic Christianity as a singular noun is a misnomer. Historically there were really Celtic Christianities, plural, each a little different from one another. Think about the diversity of Christian churches today, the vast range from fundamentalists to liberal and progressive thinkers! Ancient Celtic Christianity had a similar broad range of beliefs, doctrines, and practices, grown across centuries as well as across various lands.

Today, there's a tendency to lump all Christians together into one category—and often that category is the one that's most vocal politically and in the media. Add to that atrocities that have been done in Jesus's name down through the ages, and its no wonder that some people's first reaction when they hear I'm a Christian is to put up their defenses, assuming that I'm there to push my beliefs down their throats.

So I want to be clear about what I believe it means to follow Jesus. For me, faith is more a way of life than a set of beliefs. I sense within myself the presence of God, always there with me, my most intimate companion, closer than friends or family. That inner sense of Presence flows outward in what I call "living the compassion of Christ."

By that I don't mean asking, "What would Jesus do?" but rather, "What is Jesus doing?" In the form of Spirit, Christ is alive, in human hearts, caring about every human being. The historical foundation for that inward experience lies in the Gospel stories, which tell that Jesus lived a perfect life, that he died to show God's love for humanity, that he descended into Hell and defeated evil, and that he came back to life again so he can live inside each one of us.

Going back to that whole talk of adventure, there's a scripture that says, "If God is for us who can be against us?" (Romans 8:31). With that assurance, I can live with a little bit of recklessness. I don't have to go through life being cautious, thinking, "Oh no, something will go wrong, I'd better not try that!" Knowing that Christ inhabits my being gives me a boldness I wouldn't have otherwise.

My faith doesn't mean I expect things will always go my way, though. I don't think it guarantees me special material blessings. I will still suffer now and then because I live in a world that is difficult. But God gives me strength and peace, no matter what I'm going through—not only for myself, but also so that I can share it with others.

The concept of sharing and giving is basic to Christianity. Unfortunately, a lot of people have gotten confused about that. At this point, I often don't like to even identify with the word "Christian," because the word no longer communicates what the Jesus-way-of-life is. So if I say I'm Christian, I have to clarify that I'm a Celtic Christian—though most folks have no idea what that means—or I say I'm a progressive Christian, which defines it, or I just say I'm a follower of Jesus, which I hope doesn't have all the ugly baggage as "Christian." I feel as though before I could ever use the word "Christian" for myself again, we would have to rebrand it.

Lilly

I too face misunderstanding whenever I identify my spiritual beliefs. A lot of people, when they hear the word "Pagan," instantly think, "Satanist." Nothing could be further from the truth. The word "pagan" actually comes from *paganus*, a Latin term that referred to people with a connection to a specific area of land. Pagans of all kinds, though, have had gone through a couple thousand years of media-smear—and as a result, many people don't have any idea what Pagans really believe.

The early Roman church, in an effort to stamp out the Celtic Paganism that threatened its power, decided to cast a dark shadow over the Celts' Horned God, Cernunnos, Lord of the Wild, the Lord of Nature, the natural world unruled by human hand. Up until that point, the biblical Satan had never been described as having horns, nor were horns considered particularly evil. In fact, in some translations of the Jewish scripture, when Moses came down from Mount Sinai, he's described as wearing horns as a symbol of Divine glory. In many Pagan traditions, the bearing of horns by a Deity is a symbol of enlightenment similar to the Christian image of the halo. But when the Roman church encountered Celtic Paganism, they cast Cernunnos as the Devil, and after that, Satan was portrayed as a horned being. Satan is not, however, and never has been a part of the Celtic pantheon of Deities!

The Roman church did whatever it could to undermine and literally demonize its competition—and it was quite successful. It blamed horrific atrocities on the followers of the old traditions. It created an atmosphere where public fear and hysteria ran like wild fire. Bad things always happen in life—people die, children get sick, crops fail, and cows go dry—but if you can blame all that on your neighbor who may be a witch, it gives you someone to blame. At the same time, though, it scares you, so you turn to the church for protection against this terrible evil that's threatening your home and family. If anyone tried to speak up on behalf of reason and tolerance, the church would instantly brand him or her as a witch as well.

There were also purely practical, monetary reasons for pointing your finger at your neighbor: the accuser got a portion of the accused person's wealth, while the rest went to the church. During the Middle Ages, being a witch hunter was a lucrative business. And not a single individual accused of witchcraft was ever found innocent, regardless of evidence, rank, wealth, or standing.

Kenneth and I have both mentioned that the Pagan Celts lacked a written history. This began with the Druids' prohibition of writing, but later, there was another reason for the oral transmission of our beliefs: to protect us from persecution. Something that was written down could be used as proof against us.

Starting in the 1480s and extending into the 1750s, this persecution was sanctioned, encouraged, and even sponsored by both the church and government. "Witch" became a catchall term for anyone who refused to tow the church's line. Whether you were an herbalist, a midwife, a follower of the old religious traditions, a homosexual, a heretic, or a dissenter of any kind, you were branded as a witch. This meant you would be arrested, tortured, and then hung, drowned, or burned—and sometimes all three. By the end of three centuries of mass hysteria, some forty to a hundred thousand women, men, and children had been killed as witches. Even in the twentieth century, it was still punishable under British law to practice anything that smacked of the old ways; the Witchcraft Acts were not repealed until the 1950s.

So you can understand why Paganism was primarily an oral tradition. In a world where literacy was uncommon, this tendency became even more pronounced. In recent years, we have made a conscious effort to remedy that, but many hundreds of years of fear and secrecy leave their legacy.

At the same time, there's something wonderful about the spoken word. Our modern culture has lost that sense; we're so focused on the Internet, on e-mail and texting, that we've forgotten the power of the human voice to convey meaning that is constantly nuanced and relevant. Oral tradition is alive, growing, evolving, but as soon as something is written down and published, it ceases to evolve in that particular form. It may be picked up and given life again, but as long as it sits only on the page, it has become static, frozen. Obviously, books and other forms of recorded words can be valuable storehouses of knowledge—but unless that knowledge becomes personal, lived out by breathing, talking individuals, it becomes a dead thing.

I realize this is a very different perspective from that which most Christians have. Christianity is a religion based on a book—the Bible—but Pagan tradition is rooted in oral tradition, knowledge that has been passed from person to person for centuries. That means we don't refer to something that's orthodox and something that isn't. We have no written scriptures saying, "Believe this but don't believe that." Many Christians find that kind of flexibility hard to understand.

When it comes to the Christian church's perspective on Paganism, not a whole lot has changed over the centuries. As a practicing Celtic Pagan, I continue to run into prejudice and misunderstanding. And yet my spirituality—part of an ancient tradition that reaches back to the pre-Christian Celts—remains deep and meaningful. From the time I was a child, my most immediate experience with the Divine has been through Nature. So the term Pagan, "of the Earth," is a good fit for me. I try to see the negative reactions I encounter as opportunities to offer a wider perspective.

Most important, as a practicing Pagan I come back again and again to the concept of immanence and relationship. For me, the Deities are my constant companions. They are my friends, my teachers, my companions. They are there to give me a swift kick in the butt when

I fall short, and then pick me up when I fall down. They whisper in my ear when I need a little encouragement or a little bit of wisdom; they listen to me when I gripe about something. In return I offer them my service, my love, my dedication. They are always present in my life; I am constantly amazed by how physically they manifest at times.

Brigid is important to me in this way, as is my own personal Goddess, the Morrigan, the Celtic Goddess of war and fertility. Morrigan's worship has existed for thousands of years, but she is not your typical Deity by any stretch of the imagination. She has pushed me harder and farther, and taught me more than any other being I've ever encountered. Although she is a real pain in the butt, I love her dearly! I find her as powerful, as meaningful, and as alive in my life as megalithic humans must have.

Every time I have hit a wall in my life, if I turn to her, a door opens. I remember one time there was a mix-up with our taxes, and suddenly the IRS went in and took thousands of dollars from our account. I was freaking out, absolutely freaking out. As I drove up the street in my car one day, I prayed, "Please, please, Lady. I need help." Suddenly, a raven (the Morrigan's sacred animal) appeared in front of my windshield—literally, a foot in front of my windshield—and then it flew in front of me the length of the entire street where I was driving. As I reached the end of the street, my cell phone rang. When I answered, I heard our tax advocate say, "All the money is back in your account."

The Morrigan helped me again a couple weeks ago when I hit another wall in my life. I needed a place to live, and I said, "I need help." Within forty-five minutes, I'd found the house I needed.

So many times when I have been thinking about something, worrying about something, struggling about something, somebody suddenly speaks to me with the voice of the Divine. I can feel it and hear it to my core, and it changes everything. Experiences like this make my faith real. They take faith out of the mind and into the heart and soul. My faith isn't based merely on ideas that appeal to me; it's experiential living. These experiences allow me to feel constantly in relationship with the Divine.

I find the Divine manifesting through everything, through everybody—and I am reminded that we are never alone. Whether we are Christian or Pagan, I believe the Divine is always there in one form or another to comfort, support, teach, and challenge us to go beyond our limited understanding of things, to come closer to that luminous infinite Presence.

Kenneth

Here again, Lilly and I find common ground. I wish all people of faith could see past their differences enough to recognize that "different" does not mean "evil"! As a follower of Jesus, I feel great sorrow for the many atrocities that have been done in the name of Christ. Christianity has often strayed far, far from the path that Jesus walked.

It may have first gotten off track when the Roman Empire legally converted to Christianity. At that point, Christianity and the government joined hands for the first time (but not the last). The church and Imperial power now looked much the same: standardized, rigid, institutionalized, using coercion to enforce its power.

The Christianity of Patrick and other Celtic Christians, however, had room within it for fresh new expressions of faith. Just as illuminated Gospels like the Book of Kells enriched the Bible with the Celts' unique visual patterns, the Celts infused Christianity with a new and dynamic flavor. Patrick and those who came after him, including Brigid, planted faith communities in the style of the older Jesus movement—organically, with an allowance for creativity and diversity, encouraging new converts to work out the implications of the gospel message for themselves in particular and individual ways within their own indigenous towns and tribes.

Dara Molloy, a modern-day Irish monk on Inishmore Island, tells how in ancient times, young people, if they felt drawn to a deeply spiritual life, would go on an *imrana*—a journey on foot or horseback or by boat around the coast and back and forth between Wales, Ireland, and Scotland—in order to visit different Christian communities. These seekers would live for weeks or months in various places, where they would see how each community practiced the Jesus path. A spiritual seeker could spend years going around like this until he or she found the right place and said, "This fits me; this is me." When that finally happened, there the person would stay and settle down. The place that was congruent with each individual's soul became that person's "place of resurrection," the unique piece of Earth where they would live and die—and expect to be raised at the end of time.

Those of us who try to be faithful to Celtic Christian traditions do our best to be like those long-ago spiritual seekers who were willing to leave the familiar and seek out their individual truth. Faithfulness means asking questions: "What is our time and place all about? What is the tone of our culture? And what do these gospel stories bring to that? How do we live the gospel within our own place and time?"

So, if there is a single Celtic Christian tradition, then it tells us that we have to keep reinventing it. We have to be open to hearing new voices. We need to keep being creative and making our faith new.

Lilly

Becoming attuned to your own path, your individual way of seeking and finding the Divine, is key to Celtic spirituality. The spiritual voyage or quest as a way to find your own personal meaning is a very ancient tradition that goes way, way back, long before Christianity ever reached Britain. It's a tradition still practiced among some Celtic Pagans today.

The ancient Pagan Celts had many Deities, which meant they also had many different ways of practicing their spirituality—and many different ways of connecting with the Divine. They knew that the community and the nature of that community shaped each being, while at the same time each remained true to its unique individuality.

This means that even today, as we talk about Paganism, we need to remember we're using a very broad term that encompasses many individual ways of belief. It applies to any tradition that honors the Earth as an aspect of the Divine. A lot of traditions all over the world fit within that category; not only are there Celtic Pagans, but there are also Norse, Hindu, Native American, Greek, Slavic, Egyptian, Gypsy, and Wiccan traditions (to name only a handful).

This contributes to the wide range of beliefs encompassed by the term "Paganism." We often say, "Ask three Pagans the same question, and you'll get five answers!" And yet there are commonalities within Paganism's wide scope.

Besides the sense of spiritual connection with the Earth, another strand that runs through all Paganism is the concept of immanence—that the Divine is revealed all around us in the ordinary world. Celtic tradition—and Pagan tradition in general—recognizes and honors all the ways in which the Divine manifests. Because the Divine is so all-encompassing, it is revealed in many, many forms. It manifests through many Deities, and each of these Deities is an aspect of that infinite Spirit beyond. This belief is what makes Paganism pantheistic and polytheistic.

Each of these Deities becomes a doorway into the infinite, just as Christians often speak of Christ as a door. Our Deities all reflect aspects of the Infinite—the Divine—in a way that allows us to take something so vast and unknowable, so numinous and ineffable, and make it personal and accessible. This is what Brigid does for those of us who identify ourselves as Celtic Pagans. She is one way the Divine is revealed to us.

Some Pagans see the Deities as manifestations of the vast One, while others think of them as individual Deities. Personally, I relate to the different Deities as manifestations of the single Infinite that's beyond name, beyond comprehension. As both Kenneth and I have said, though, the Celts have a great respect for spiritual differences, and they honor each individual's journey to a personal truth. For me, the way in which truth reaches us as individuals is an example of the Divine's enormous compassion, providing so many gateways into itself for the infinite varieties of human personality and need.

The wheel cross—the equal-arm cross—is the Pagan symbol of our connection with something beyond ourselves. It represents the path we walk in our lives toward unity with the Infinite. For Pagans all over the world this cross symbolizes the four elements. The center represent the soul, the Divine center within each of us, and each arm of the cross indicates a different element. Within my own Pagan tradition, we see the eastern arm as wind, symbolizing the mind, our thought processes, and the search for knowledge. The southern arm is fire, a symbol for the body; it represents our passion and purpose in life, our driving force. The western arm is the flowing of water, representing our heart, our emotions. Last, the northern arm is the Earth—the Spirit from which all things spring and come together. In the end, we return to the Earth, to the Spirit.

Kenneth

In fact, the wheel cross symbol is almost synonymous with Celtic identity. This ancient design goes back deep into the long-ago, to the pre-Celtic shape of the Callanish Stone Circle in the Hebrides, erected a millennia before the Celts arrived. For Celtic Christians, the wheel cross expresses the totality of the cosmos.

As Lilly's comments indicate, Celtic spirituality does not separate Spirit and Earth, the way our Western thinking does. We inherited this dualistic thinking from the pre-Christian Greeks and Romans, but the ancient Celts had a different way of looking at life. When Celts converted to Christianity, they brought this holistic perspective with them. They perceived the entirety of ordinary daily life as being encompassed in the redeeming work of Christ—and the wheel cross was the visual representation of this.

Of course, the cross for Celtic Christians also has the same primary significance that it has for all Christians: it is both the symbol of Christ's death and a reminder of the way in which he spanned the gap between God and humanity. It is the visual representation of 2 Corinthians 5:19, which says, "God was in Christ reconciling the world to God's self."

The ancient Celtic saints, however, saw the significance of the cross from a different perspective from that of most modern Christians. Today, most churches teach that Christ died to appease God the Father's discontent with the world, a view known as "substitutionary atonement": Christ substituted himself for human beings, so that we would not need to bear God's wrath. This isn't the way Celtic saints looked at the cross, though. Instead, they adhered to another view called *Christus Victor*, which emphasized Christ's entry through the cross to the Devil's realm, where Christ the Hero defeated evil and death. A modern illustration of the Celtic concept of Christus Victor is in Tolkien's Lord of the Rings trilogy, when Gandalf falls into the depths of the earth battling the demon Balrog, only to emerge alive again and victorious.

Ultimately, though, as Lilly has pointed out, the wheel cross in the British Isles was historically pre-Christian. It's another example of the way in which ancient elements of Celtic spirituality blended easily with Christianity when it arrived in Celtic lands.

In fact, the circle with a cross within it is a meaningful symbol for many cultures around the world. For the Celts, the eightfold seasons of the year also formed a wheel, with quarterly celebrations between solstices creating cross arms that look very much like the Buddhist dharma wheel, another interesting congruity between spiritual traditions. In North America, the Lakota medicine wheel is still another example of a wheel cross.

Lilly

I've heard that there was a prophecy among one of the Native American tribes that there would be people who came from across the ocean bearing a cross. If they carried the equal-arm cross, all would be well. But if they came with a cross with odd-lengthed arms, they would bring fire and destruction. Celtic Christianity's encounter with Native beliefs in the Americas would have turned out much differently, I believe, from what often happened when the institutionalized church interacted with indigenous beliefs.

My own heritage is Native American—Blackfoot and Cherokee—as well as Scottish and German. (I'm an American mutt!) Early in my spiritual journey, I studied Native American traditions. When I turned to Celtic spirituality, I found so many similarities between these traditions.

Truly, though, if you seek out the heart and core of any religion, you'll find we are all speaking of the same things. Our language and our symbols for the mysteries may be different, but the mysteries themselves are the same. Truth is truth, and love is love, no matter what face or name you give to it. As a Pagan, Brigid is one of the many faces that reveal Divine love to me.

2

Meeting Brigid

Lilly

I stand at the bottom of a hollow, deep in the woods, a sword strapped to my side. A path stretches out before and behind me. I am surrounded by the green darkness of forest, but ahead of me, as the path climbs the hill, I see light through the trees. My footsteps echo in the quiet as I climb the slope and then emerge from the trees into an open area. Framed in the arch of the last trees is a standing stone. The stone is ancient, cup-marked and spiraled. Etched clearly near its base is the image of the triskelion, the image of the Celtic triple Goddess.

As I kneel to look closer at the markings of the stone, I hear a rustle in the grass. I rise, and Brigid steps out from behind the ancient stone. She is beautiful, neither young nor old, timeless and ageless. Her cloak is the green of spring grass, and her hair is the color of flames. I greet her with warmth and familiarity, for we have met many times before. In fact, the sword I wear was her gift to me.

"Look," she says to me now as she gestures with her hand. I see that laid out below this hilltop is a beautiful valley. The path meanders down the hill ahead of me and then through the valley, fading off into the distance.

As I stand there, the sun warm on my face, her presence and the beauty that lies ahead combine to give me a sense of hope and peace. When I look back over my shoulder at the path I have just traveled, back into the darkness beneath the trees, I realize I have left fear and sorrow behind me in those thick woods. I have hardly been aware of their weight upon my soul, but now, here in Brigid's presence, I feel them lift, leaving me lighter and freer.

"Do you see?" Brigid asks me. "You have come out of the woods. Now it is time to leave those sorrows behind. You have much joy and abundance still ahead of you in this life."

I realize I am standing at the threshold of a new cycle. She gestures to the sword I carry on my hip, a gift of her forge. "Do you remember the power of this sword?" she asks.

I nod. "It has the ability to separate truth from illusion."

"And did you think you could hold on to illusion and not be cut by it?"

I know she is referring to the way I have been holding on to a relationship that has clearly ended. Filled with sorrow, I shake my head.

"You have to release the illusions of the past," she tells me, "before you will be able to embrace the present and continue on your path. If you cling to old pain, you will remain lost in the woods. If you refuse to release your expectations, you will remain wandering and confused. The more you hold on to these illusions, the more you will be cut by them."

As she speaks, clarity cuts through the pain and confusion I have been carrying. It falls away from me, like a dead skin.

She smiles. "One more thing—when you write, share not only my history, but also who I am in the present. I offer you my blessing for your work and endeavors."

Warmth and peace flow through me. She beckons me to follow her, and I take another step forward, away from the shadows. . . . When I return to physical awareness, the sense of absolute clarity remains with me, along with the lingering warmth of Brigid's presence. The sorrow and confusion I have been struggling with have lifted.

What I have just described is a shamanic journey, a practice that uses deep trance work to shift our consciousness in order to access other realms, non-ordinary states of reality. It is a tool for spiritual development and healing, one that has deep and abiding effects. The language of shamanic journeys is at the same time both literal and symbolic, a way to go deep into the psyche to face conscious and unconscious aspects of ourselves. As a result, we are freed to grow and transform.

As a shamanic healer, I collaborate closely and personally with several Deities. Brigid is one of the ones I work with most frequently, both in my practice and in my personal life. The kind of interaction I just described can be a daily occurrence, and the Deities' comfort and guidance offer me a constant source of insight and wisdom.

But I didn't always have the relationship with Brigid that I have today. Years ago, when I began to delve into

Celtic Pagan tradition, I first encountered her as a form of the Pagan Triple Goddess. Celtic Pagans honor the Goddess in her triple aspect, represented by the three stages of a woman's life: maiden, mother, and crone. Another way to look at these three Divine aspects is creation, preservation, and destruction or deconstruction. (This very closely parallels the Hindu concept of the Divine having three persons: Brahma, the creator; Vishnu, the maintainer or preserver; and Shiva, the destroyer or transformer. Each of these Hindu Gods also has a feminine counterpart—Saraswati, Lakshmi, and Durga—who are coexistent with them.)

So this was my first concept of Brigid—as a form of the Triple Goddess, whose symbol is the waxing, full, and waning moon. As Anne Ross says in her book *Pagan Celtic Britain,*

> The basic Celtic Goddess type was at once mother, warrior, hag, virgin, conveyor of fertility . . . giver of prosperity to the land, protectress of the flock and herds. More static and more archaic than the gods, she remained tied to the land for which she was responsible and whose most striking natural features seemed to her worshippers to be manifestations of her power and personality.

My curiosity about Brigid was aroused, but I still had not truly made her acquaintance.

Later, I moved to Britain, where I found her influence and presence again and again in the names of holy wells and springs, in the iconography of churches, in the stories and lore that the very land itself seemed to exude. At this point, my relationship with her was one of curiosity and polite interest, the way you might feel about some prominent person in the neighborhood, someone you've heard a lot of positive things about though you don't know her personally.

Then, as I continued more deeply into my studies of Celtic Paganism and my exploration of the land itself, Brigid's presence became more and more obvious and influential in my life. Eventually, she came to be one of the most transformational Goddesses in my life. Many years ago, after I came to know her better, she offered me her help, not only for my own healing but also as a catalyst within my practice for healing others.

So when I speak of Brigid, I'm not referring only to a historical person or a mythological Deity but also to a being who is very much present in my day-to-day life. My interactions with her have shaped and formed my spiritual path in more ways than I can possibly count. She is not a storybook character but a real being who is always evolving and growing. The more I relate to her that way, the more intimate my relationship with her becomes—and the more light she sheds on my consciousness.

As we turn to Brigid's story, keep in mind her living presence in the here-and-now. As you learn about the historical and cultural context of her past, allow that to enrich your understanding of her present being.

Brigid's influence has been one of the most long-lived and far reaching of the Celtic Deities'. The Pagan Celts had several hundred Deities, and most of them were very localized, connected to individual tribes' specific lands or ancestors. Brigid, however, is one of the few Goddesses who span all of Celtic Paganism across a vast period of time.

She has had slightly different names, however, at various times and in various places. The Irish knew her as Brigid, Bride, or Breed; she was Brigantia among the British; and Brigindo and Minerva Belisima in Gaul. She was later known as Saint Brigit in Ireland, Saint Ffraid in Wales, and Saint Bride in Scotland. Over the years, she has also been known as Brigit, Brigid, Bhrighde, Brida, Brid, Brigh, Breeshey, Brittania, and Brigandu. Her name may come from the Gaelic word *breo-aigit,* meaning "fiery arrow." For the Irish, *brig* meant "power or craft," while the Welsh *bri* meant "honored and reknown."

Brigid was first mentioned in the Leabhor Gabhala Erenn (the Irish Book of Invasions), one of our few remaining early texts of Celtic history, spirituality, and mythology. The Leabhor Gabhala records the invasions and settling of Ireland by various tribes of people. The Tuatha De Danaan (Children of Danu)—sometimes called the Ever-Living Ones—were one of the last of these groups of settlers, a race of god-like magical beings. Danu was their great Mother Goddess, and Dagda—"the Good God"—was their father God. Brigid was said to be the daughter of Danu and Dagda, making her a powerful figure in the Tuatha De Dannan. When the Mileasians, a Celtic tribe from the Iberian Peninsula of Spain, supplanted the Tuatha De Danaan, they retreated into the Sidhe—the Celtic Other World. From there they continued to influence Celtic life, becoming some of the early Gods of the Irish.

Our next references to Brigid come from the tales and myths of the early Celts as written down by Christian monks. As Pagans, we are grateful that these books exist—that the monks preserved for us knowledge that would otherwise have been lost to us as the Druids died out—but it is always a challenge to sift through the Christian overlay on the old stories to find the true heart and core of the ancient traditions.

In these tales, Brigid appears in several roles. She is spoken of sometimes as the daughter of the Morrigan and sometimes as the daughter of Boann, Goddess of the river Boyne in Ireland. Within these variations, we see a common deep connection to the earth and waters, as well as allusions that point to Brigid's sovereignty. Her being is related to light and the returning of the sun at Imbolc (the halfway point between the winter solstice and the spring equinox). According to legend, she was raised on the milk of a white cow with red ears. (Celtic tradition believed that white-bodied, red-eared animals belonged to the Sidhe—the Fey or Fairy folk.) The colors white and red are still considered sacred to Brigid in her many forms.

As Ken mentioned earlier, we Celts love to look at the world in sets of three. Brigid too has a triple aspect: she is the Goddess of hearth and home; the Goddess of smithcraft; and the Goddess of Divine inspiration. Note that each of these three aspects all relate to fire: the hearth fire, the forge fire, and the flame of inspiration. Brigid is also sometimes referred to as the three daughters of the Dagda, each of the daughters being called Brigid and each having one of the aspects and skills with which Brigid as a single Goddess is attributed.

Brigid's triple nature connected her to some of the most vital pieces of Celtic life. As the Goddess of hearth and home, she played an important role in healing and midwifery, as well as the herds and animal husbandry. She had particular connections to milk and wool, vital resources for sustaining the tribe through the lean times of late winter. As the Goddess of Divine inspiration, she was regarded as a muse who brought words and knowledge. People turned to her as a source of divination and prophecy, and poets often considered themselves to be her sons and daughters.

As with many Deities, her stories and influence evolved and spread over time and distance. The Roman invasion of Britain did nothing to destroy her influence, since the Romans quickly adopted her as Dea Brigantia, associating her with their own Goddess Athena.

The Romans, by the way, were often very clever in their conquests of new territories. When they invaded and conquered a new land, rather than destroying the local Deities—which would have caused uproar and incited resistance—they would simply identify the local Deities with ones from their Roman pantheon. Then they could slowly absorb the Deities and their followers into Roman culture, melding Pagan and Roman traditions together. For the most part this worked well, although in some areas the Druids were not so easily controlled. Unfortunately, where this was the case, the Romans were merciless; they slaughtered the rebellious Druids, destroyed their sacred groves, and wiped out their traditions.

But while Brigid's influence may have faded a little in Roman-occupied Britain and Wales, it continued as strongly as ever in Ireland and Scotland. In a culture that counted wealth not in coin but in heads of cattle or other livestock, the protection and fertility of the herds and flocks was vital to the community. Brigid's connection to livestock gave her a profound importance, and she became even more popular than many of the other Deities in the Celtic pantheon, a popularity that continued right up into more modern times.

Was there a historical, "factual" Brigid who formed the foundation of all our stories about the Goddess? As Celtic Pagans, we don't need to know. We know that story is often more "true" than fact. Story can reveal a deeper reality. Within this spiritual realm is where we encounter Brigid, and it is from here that she continues to bless and give meaning to our lives.

Kenneth

Story also reveals the meaning of the Christian Brigid. This Brigid came into being more recently than her Pagan counterpart, and so we are able to discern through the mists of time a few historical facts—but the lines between history and legend are blurred.

The legends that surround Brigid are similar to the traditions surrounding King Arthur: a historical person lies at the core, with myths and legends woven around that individual. In Arthur's case, it's likely there really was a Welsh warlord who fought off the Saxons in the sixth century—but then storytellers took accounts of the old Celtic Gods and wove them into stories of Arthur and his knights. So we really can't tell anymore what is myth and what is historical fact because they're so entangled. The same sort of thing has happened with Brigid. What shines out clearly, however, is the brightness of Brigid's personality and life. Like the Goddess Brigid, Saint Brigid was a being who shed great light.

According to one version of the Christian legend, because Brigid had been born out of wedlock, her stern tribesmen disapproved of her very existence—and so, hours after her birth, they set her adrift in a tiny hide-covered coracle. The waves and the wind carried her across the Irish Sea to the Holy Island of Iona. Centuries later, this island would become famous for Saint Colmkille (Columba), who declared, "Christ is my Druid." But in Brigid's time, it was still the sacred island of the Druids themselves, the Celts' white-robed priests. The Druids raised Brigid to know all their vast store of knowledge—to know herself a part of the wind, the waves, the soil, the flocks, the wells, the rain, and the sun.

Brigid could swim with the seals, her spirit soared with the gulls, and she loved to ramble across the island with the gentle sheep. Craving the company of creatures and green things, she often wandered in Nature's solitude. As she grew into a young woman, there was something about her that impressed all who knew her. Her words struck truer, her eyes glowed brighter, her hair shone redder, and her soul leapt out of her like none of her companions.

One cold night, Brigid climbed the tall hill that overlooked the beach, from which she could look across the water to the larger island of Mull. Far below, near their stone huts, she could see her fellow Druids setting a log afire and gathering around it to celebrate *Mean Geimredh*, the longest night of the year. Part of her wanted to scramble down the hill and join the celebration—but it was too dark to descend safely, and besides, she felt very, very weary. So she curled up in a hollow on the hilltop and drifted into sleep.

As she slept, the images that came into her head were so vivid and tangible, she couldn't be certain if she dreamed or was awake. She found herself in a hot, dry place, not at all like the cold wet grass on Iona where she had fallen asleep. The air carried strange, pungent scents, the aromas of spices and flowers she'd never smelled before.

She entered a little house made of clay, with many rooms and blankets covering the doors. Inside was an old man, coarse and gruff, with dark hair, dark eyes, and brown skin. "No more guests tonight!" he shouted when he saw her, as though he thought she were his servant. "We have three, four bodies in every room. There isn't a space to lay a stick between them. So don't waste time on these travelers come from the census—just tell them loud and plain, 'There is no room for you at this inn tonight!' You hear me?"

Too confused to ask questions, Brigid simply nodded.

"Good!" the man barked and disappeared through one of the doors.

No sooner had he departed than she heard a knock on the door that led outdoors. She opened it and found a thin, straggly-haired man holding a donkey by a rope. A young woman was seated on the donkey, her belly so round and full that Brigid thought a baby would pop out of it any moment.

"Please," the man said, "we are tired and hungry. My wife Miriam is about to have our baby. Can you give us a room for the night?"

Brigid felt an awful weight crushing down on her, as if the very universe cried out for mercy on this mother and her unborn child. Yet what could she do? Even if she were to disobey the man who had assumed she was his servant, he had said there was literally no room for another traveler—and certainly not for a pregnant woman who was likely to give birth at any moment.

As Brigid stood hesitating in the door, she noticed a dirt track that led to an animal shed beyond the inn. At least, she thought, its enclosure would be warmer than the night air, and there would be straw there to make a bed for the woman.

"Come with me," she told the man. She led them to the shed, shooed a few chickens and ducks out of the way, and nudged a cow to move over and make room for the donkey. Then she arranged hay for a bed. The young woman gave her a grateful smile and sank down on the straw with a sigh.

Brigid hated to leave her. She watched as the woman's hands clutched her belly and her back arched. After a moment she relaxed again, but before long, she gasped as a new pain gripped her. The woman was already in labor, Brigid realized; she couldn't leave her now.

The husband fidgeted and looked desperate. Brigid took his elbow and gently pushed him over to stand beside the cow and the donkey, where he would be out of the way. Then she knelt beside the woman, murmuring comforting words. Brigid had been taught midwifery, and she knew what needed to be done.

Several hours later, Brigid received the newborn baby into her arms. She carefully cut his cord and wrapped him up tight and warm in her own mantle. The young woman gave her an exhausted smile, then turned to look up at her husband.

Brigid knew from experience that when a birth goes right, it's always a moment of great joy—but somehow she sensed that this birth was more special than any other she had seen. The very air seemed to ring with a silent message: "This is no ordinary child. This is the

Master of the Elements—the great Life that gives Life to all lives. This helpless wee bairn is the Light come into the long night of the darkened world."

The young mother held her baby to her breast, but after a moment, she let out a soft cry of despair. She was utterly spent, Brigid realized, too weary after the long hours of labor to be able to suckle her baby. The woman looked up at Brigid, and tears of exhaustion spilled out of her eyes. "God help me," she whispered. "How can I find the strength for my little one?"

Brigid felt a warm tingling in her own breasts, and to her amazement, she realized her body was ready to feed the newborn baby. She gathered him up into her arms and suckled him as the father and mother fell into exhausted sleep.

And as she nursed the baby, Brigid experienced the oddest sensation: she felt as if her soul expanded and blazed with warmth, as if she herself were the longest night of the year and now the Light was streaming out from her to illumine the world. As her milk nourished the Master of the Elements, so his Life flowed back into her.

From that day on, Bride became the living image of compassion. Never again would she even consider turning a single soul away from her door. No person who came to her seeking help or wisdom or sympathy would ever be refused.

And so Brigid became known as the Foster Mother of Christ, not only because of her visionary experience—which may or may not have happened—but because she nourished the message of Christ in her heart and then carried it to her people. She had truly opened her arms to Jesus, and she would never again put him down.

Many Celtic Christians believe that Brigid carries on her work as the Christ-bearer even after her death. When people are on the point of "losing their religion"—when the husband is ready to yell at the wife, and the wife is ready to snarl at her child, and the child is about to kick the poor dog—they need only call upon Brigid. When they do, the compassion and peace of the All-Healer is restored to their hearts and home.

I heard this story while I was on a retreat with Fionn Tulach, Abbess of the Ce'ili De' Scottish monastic order. It was a lengthy and mesmerizing tale, told by candlelight, that began with the same story Lilly has told, describing Brigid's life as one of the Sidhe. Fionn used the Scots' Gaelic name "Bride," however, instead of "Brigid," and her version went on to describe the Goddess's Christian incarnation. This latter part of the tale is what I have just related from memory. (I am sure my rendition differs more than a little from Fionn Tulach's version, but that's acceptable and good. Such is the way of a story: each teller adds a piece of himself, so that the story becomes ongoing and animated.)

Turning from story to history, here's what we know: somewhere around the year 453, an Irish lass was born and named Brigid. Innumerable other women would have been named after the Goddess too, similar to the way that so many Irish women have been named Mary since Christianity came to Ireland.

According to another story, when Brigid's mother, a bondswoman, was nine months pregnant, her master summoned her early one morning, while it was still dark. As she rushed to obey, she tripped on the threshold of her little house. Her water broke as she fell—and suddenly she knew her baby was coming *now*! She squatted half in and half out of the door to her house—and just as the sun rose, Brigid was born right there, on the threshold.

This story is full of symbolism. Celtic spirituality—be it Christian or Pagan—recognizes the holiness of liminal space. Liminal space is what lies between two other points, neither one thing or another. Between number one and number two, for example, you have an infinite number of fractions. These "points between" are liminal space. Fog is liminal because it separates light and dark, vision and unseeing, so the Celts considered mist to always be a sacred threshold. Pools and wells were sacred thresholds between the underworld and this world. Mountains were thresholds between this world and the sky world. All these in-between places were holy ground. So when Brigid was born on a threshold, at the moment between day and night, it was a strong portent that symbolically foretold two aspects of her life.

First, her life was lived out in the space between eras, between Paganism and Christianity, a time of immense transition. Her life bridged both traditions. She was born on the threshold between two modes of spirituality.

Second, Brigid lived her life in the liminal space between Heaven and Earth. The Celts perceived liminal spaces as "thin places" where the supernatural world and the visible world could meet, allowing beings to pass back and forth from one to the other. Throughout Brigid's life, she held a thin place within her own self. She was rooted in the practical everyday world, but she could also see the world of angels and spirits. Her life was lived on the threshold.

At the same time that Brigid was growing up, Patrick was wandering back and forth across Ireland, teaching everyone about Jesus of Nazareth. At some point, Brigid became another of his converts. The next certain historical fact in Brigid's life comes when she founded her monastery at Kildare.

This had once been a Druid center of learning, one of the great centers of druidic lore. We don't know how the transition came about, but by the year 480, Kildare had become Brigid's monastery, a Christian community. Kildare comes from the same word root as *druid*; the Druids were "oak wise," and *kildare* meant "church of the oak" in Irish Gaelic. Oak trees were believed to be portals between natural and supernatural realms—another liminal space—so for Brigid to choose this location for her monastery may indicate that her roots in her Druid past remained deep and strong.

It seems likely that Brigid may have first been a leader of the Druid community at Kildare. The others in the community would have respected her wisdom and strong spiritual and magical powers—so when she embraced the new faith, they did the same. This nearly invisible transition from a Druid community to a Christian monastery, one building on the other, is typical of early Celtic spirituality. The change did not involve war, conquest, violence, or suppression. The community had been focused on one form of spirituality, and now it focused on another form, but the deep spirituality remained.

However it happened, Kildare became a Christian monastery with Brigid as its abbess. It was a mixed-gender monastery, as was common with the ancient Irish Christians (though not so much for the Scots and Welsh). For the most part, these Celtic monasteries were quite different from the exclusively male Roman-style monasteries. An early Irish monastery would be a Christian community made up of families—typically, several hundred people in all—creating a kind of holy village where life revolved around daily worship.

Brigid may have also been a bishop (as well as an abbess). This would now be unusual in many Christian traditions, but the pre-Christian Celts had an egalitarian perspective on gender roles. Anything a man could do, a woman could do; being a landowner or a leader were roles open to women as much as to men. So it seems likely that the story that Brigid was a bishop holds historical truth. As this early stage in Ireland's Christianity, there were two Irish bishops: in the north, was Patrick, the first bishop of Ireland, while Brigid functioned as bishop in southern Ireland.

A statue at Cashel gives us evidence that at the heart of the ancient Irish ecclesial world, Brigid was regarded as an authority as great as—or even greater than—Jesus's original apostles. Cashel, the seat of the southern Irish church, still stands, and today you can still see inside the ruins of the chapel a sculpture portraying Christ's twelve apostles—and in front of the twelve, to the left of them all, is Brigid.

Brigid's influence spread from Ireland through all the Celtic lands. The Hebrides—the Isles of Bride—are named after her. She's also associated with Glastonbury, the mythic Avalon, in Somerset, at the heart of England. At the top of Glastonbury Tor stands the ancient Saint Michael's church with two sculptures. One is the angel Michael, the church's namesake, and on the other side is Brigid with her cow. Holy wells in Wales, England, and Scotland, as well as Ireland, bear Brigid's name. As we've said, the Celts, both Pagan and Christian, considered wells to be thin places, liminal spaces where people could access the spiritual world. The water from these holy wells carried Brigid's blessing and healing.

Brigid's crosses are yet another tradition that honors Brigid's memory. These crosses, made from reeds or straw, hang over the doors in many Irish homes even today to bless and protect the house. They are often created on February 1, Brigid's feast day. As with all Celtic traditions, there's a story or two behind Brigid's cross.

According to one tradition, as a chieftain who lived near Kildare was dying, members of his household sent for Brigid to comfort him with the Good News of Christ. When she arrived, however, the chieftain was so delirious he was unable to understand what she said to him. Brigid knew that sometimes an image is more powerful than any words, so she sat down at his bedside and looked around for a way to show him Jesus. As her eyes lit on the rushes strewn across the dirt floor, as was customary for warmth and cleanliness, she got an idea. She stooped down and gathered some into her lap, and then she wove them into a cross. The sick man fixed his eyes on the cross and grew calm. Brigid talked to him softly about Jesus, and the man died with a look of joy on his face.

In reality, the reed cross was probably connected with the Goddess Brigid long before Christianity came to Ireland. So we have to ask the question: did Brigid of Kildare intentionally take on herself the Goddess Brigid's stories in order to create within her life a space where

Pagans and Christians could find common ground? Whatever the truth is, it's clear that the fifth-century Brigid was an unusual woman whose light still glows, even many centuries later.

As a Protestant Christian, I was reared in traditions that don't celebrate the saints. "You only pray to Jesus," I was taught, and the concept of interacting with people who are now in Heaven was considered to be misguided, at best, and at worst, idolatry. More recently, however, I've grown into a deeper understanding of my spiritual heritage as a Celt. I don't have the kind of experiences Lilly has described, but I do sense the companionship of Brigid and other departed saints. I think of Brigid as my older sister in the faith, a companion on my journey. I sometimes ask her to pray for me, in the same way that I ask my other friends (living or departed) to pray for me. I believe she *still* occupies a liminal space between the visible and invisible worlds.

3

Brigid and the Invisible World

Lilly

When Kenneth talks about liminal space, he could be quoting one of my own lectures word for word! The concept of thin places, the space-between, is clearly one of the common threads that connect Pagan and Christian Celtic traditions.

According to Pagan traditions, Brigid was the Goddess of the crossroads, the place where the two worlds—visible and the invisible—met. The reed cross, Pagans believe, symbolizes this intersection between the worlds. It could represent the sun as well, for Brigid was also solar Goddess. February 1 was her day (just as it is the Christian saint's feast day) because it was another kind of crossroads, the turning point between the winter solstice and the spring equinox. Despite the differences between Pagan and Christian traditions, we find here another parallel between the two Brigids; both perspectives connect her with liminal space.

The Pagan Celts had the sense that other realms—the realms of the spirit—were always rubbing shoulders with the physical world. The Fey, the Sidhe, the ancestors, and the Gods were all right there with them, in the land, the water, the winds, the mist and fog. This gave the Celts the constant feeling that if you wandered off the beaten path, you might just step into the in-between and find yourself in the spirit realms. Finding your way out again—well that was the trick! Those who did were never quite the same.

The Goddess Brigid contains within herself many of the spirit realm's most potent symbols. As the Goddess of the forge, she has the power of creativity and transformation. In ancient Celtic culture (and Norse as well), smithcraft was interwoven with magic, and smiths were often seen as having mildly superhuman powers. After all, smiths took raw material from the earth and changed it into a different form, something new and useful. This meant they had mystical powers of transformation. Their role in the tribe was considered to be a sacred trust, since it required that they master the four primal elements: *fire* to heat the substance of the *earth*, and then *air* and *water* to cool their creation. In this way, they reenacted the creation of the world.

Brigid as the Mistress of the Forge plays an important role in my own spiritual practice, where I use the concept of the forge as a compelling tool, a metaphor for spiritual transformation. The raw ore of our souls enters the crucible of the spiritual journey, and there our relationship with the Divine heats and purifies the metal. The ego is burned away in the fire of our connection with the Infinite, and the strong metal of our souls can then be shaped by our life experiences. Just as iron tools are hammered hard to make them useful, life also beats on our souls—but then they are plunged into the living water, where they are cooled and nurtured. The process is repeated again and again, honing and sharpening our inner being, until the raw metal has been transformed into a perfect tool in the hands of our Gods. Meditating on Brigid's forge can give us greater endurance for the trials and tribulations we all go through in our spiritual journeys, the times when life requires that we "walk through the fire."

In my own practice, it is in Brigid's aspect as Mistress of the Forge that I most powerfully relate to her. She has great power in this guise to connect me to the invisible world of the spirit. Others, however, may relate more to another aspect of the Goddess; for example, Brigid is also the Goddess of Inspiration.

The Celts believed that language, memory, and poetry formed a three-strand braid (there's the number three again!) that was a gift from the Gods. The Druids' taboo against putting their mysteries into written form was because words were so powerful; instead, their vast collection of wisdom was often contained in the form of spoken poetry. For the Celts, poetry, storytelling, and music were all ways to tap into the invisible world and bring it out into the visible. So closely were wordcraft and the invisible world connected that the ancient Celtic word for "poetry" came from the same root as "to see." Poets—people who could shape words to tell stories, create songs, and contain knowledge—could see into the invisible world, and then reveal their vision to others through words.

Divine inspiration could create poetry that was entertaining, informative, and even dangerous. One of the worst things that could be done to a ruler, chieftain, or king was for him to be satirized by a poet or bard. If this happened due to his lack of courtesy or wisdom, the satire would spread, undermining his rule and authority; in some cases, it could literally bring about his downfall. (Today, we can see that the media often has a very similar power over politics.)

Like the Muses in Roman mythology, Brigid was the source of creative inspiration and poetry, and poets were held under her explicit protection. In this role she is pictured carrying a wand with a crescent moon and a tablet.

According to an old story, Brigid once took shelter with a chieftain and his family for the night. During dinner, she noticed harps hanging on the wall, so she asked the chieftain if his children would play for her. The chieftain responded that his children were not yet skilled enough. He apologized that he could not offer the Goddess music as entertainment, for his own bard was currently on a journey. At this, Brigid blessed the children's hands—and from that day forward, the chieftain's children played with such skill that they and their descendents became great bards and musicians for many generations after.

Some Pagans believe that poets and other wordsmiths who have gone before us inhabit the realms between the worlds, those liminal spaces that overlap with ours, where they keep the old songs and stories alive. When we think of Brigid as the Goddess of Inspiration, we can turn to her in a similar way, for continuity with the past, inspiration for the present moment, and encouragement and hope for the future. At each point, she will be there, connecting us constantly to the invisible world where we find connection with the Infinite.

Kenneth

Brigid's life reminds us that extraordinary happenings are not impossible. She offers assurance that seemingly ordinary people can be vessels of Divine power to achieve much more than they would have ever deemed possible.

And as Lilly points out, Brigid is not limited by the boundaries of time. Within the realm of eternity, she remains a living entity. Another old story underlines this belief.

A hundred years or so after the Christian Brigid's death, the community at Kildare had expanded to the point that they needed to add on to their church. As with any remodeling effort, however, there was a degree of tension between building something new while preserving meaningful pieces of the old building. In this case, no one wanted to get rid of an old door on the left side of the church through which Brigid had always entered the building. In the remodeling process, however, they had enlarged the doorway, and now, no matter how much the workmen tried, they could not get the old door to cover the new opening. And yet they hated to get rid of the door that had been touched by Brigid's actual hands.

The workmen got together to discuss what they should do. Should they make a new, larger door that would fill the entranceway properly? Or should they add a panel to the old door, even though that would change the door's character? One of the chief artisans in the community spoke up and said, "Let's ask Brigid herself what we should do. Tonight, let us join in prayer, fervently asking our Lord that by morning Brigid will give us the direction we need—that we will know clearly the right course of action to take."

That night, the artisan settled himself beside Brigid's tomb, where he passed the entire night in prayer. When morning came, he got to his feet, feeling no clearer about what to do than he had the night before. Sadly, he went to the doorway that was causing so much trouble. One more time, he put the old door into the new doorway, hoping that some new idea might occur to him in the process. Instead, when the old door had settled on its hinges, he found it filled the entire doorway. The worn wood fit the new doorframe as snugly as if it had been built for it, neither a hair too big nor a hair too small. Saint Brigid, through the power of Divine omnipotence, had fixed her door.

Miracles are part and parcel of Celtic hagiographies; there is not a single Gaelic saint who didn't perform miracles. There was biblical basis for this: Jesus had promised his followers, "I tell you the truth, anyone who believes in me will do the same works I have done, and even greater works, because I am going to be with the Father" (John 14:12 NLT). Centuries after Jesus's life on earth, in a land geographically far removed from his home turf, the stories about their saints' miracles were a way for the Celts to say, "See, we share the same Spirit as Christ and his Apostles."

I'm not saying, though, that I believe these miraculous events were all simply good stories, embellishments added later to the actual events. Columba's chronicler Adomnan, for example, was the son of his cousin; he was someone who knew Columba personally, and he would have spoken directly with people who had lived with his great-uncle—yet his work is comprised mostly of descriptions of Columba's miracles. Clearly, he believed that these events had actually transpired. Gildas, the first Saxon historian, recorded in his *Ecclessiastical History* the lives of people who were recently deceased or (in a few cases) still living, and his account also has its share of miraculous events. Gildas seems to document these especially carefully, as if he were aware that even his medieval readers would be incredulous about such matters.

In this regard, Lilly and I are closer in our beliefs than I am to some of my Christian colleagues. Lilly affirms that magic takes place, I prefer the term "miracle," but we both believe, as Hamlet said, "There are more things in heaven and earth . . . than are dreamt of in your philosophy."

A reader of my book *Water from an Ancient Well: Celtic Spirituality for Modern Life* once told me, "You seem like a very reasonable fellow—until you start talking about angels, demons, and miracles." I acknowledge that in today's world, belief in miracles can seem irrational, but I couldn't claim to be living an authentic Celtic Christian faith without some belief in the miraculous. For that matter, I don't think *any* Christian can authentically claim to be living as heir to Christ and the Apostles without placing some credence in the Spirit's powerful workings.

One thing I find fascinating about the miracles ascribed to the Celtic saints is that the kinds of feats differ from saint to saint. Miracles seem fitted to the personality of each individual. From the perspective of Christian theology, these different types of miracles might be attributed to the *charisms*—the various spiritual gifts that God gives uniquely to each individual in a way that fits that person's deep soul-identity.

While I believe that astonishing supernatural events really do occur, I also affirm a symbolic connection between the lives of individuals and the miracles they perform. Because something is a metaphor for a larger reality doesn't mean that the metaphor isn't also real! In John's Gospel, for example, every miracle described is a "sign," a "signifier" (Greek *semeion*) of something else. Miracles signify God working in the world, yet they do so through the distinctive personality of each miracle worker.

To demonstrate this, consider a few categories of miracles ascribed to Saint Brigid by her early biographers. The lion's share of her miracles are signs of compassion (recall Fionn Tulach's account of light flooding the girl Bride's soul as she nurses the Christ). As one example,

Cogitosus, writing in the seventh century, records the following:

> Brigid, drawing upon the strength of faith, blessed a woman who had taken a vow of virginity. The woman had weakened and lapsed into youthful concupiscence [aka lust], as a result of which her womb had begun to swell with pregnancy. As a result of the blessing that which had been conceived in the womb disappeared. The woman was healed without any of the pain of childbirth.

And she returned to the life she had chosen before she had gotten sidetracked. This story is a particularly interesting one in today's world where abortion is an ongoing controversial topic. Whatever implications you may draw from Brigid's actions, what's clear is that compassion was the benchmark by which she lived. Caring for another's pain—without judgment or condescension—may be the greatest power we have within us.

Another pattern we see in Brigid's miracles is the way they enable her to outwit male opponents who seemingly have more power. This is a repeated formula in the stories about Brigid: first, she challenges a male in authority, who makes her an insincere and mocking promise; then, with the assistance of a miracle, Brigid gets her desired outcome at the expense of the more powerful party. The story told earlier about how she used her mantle to get the land she wanted for her monastery is an example of this.

This type of miracle enabled Brigid to hold seemingly disparate aspects within a unified personality. She could remain humble, while at the same time trumping the power of mighty masculine monarchs. She is honest, yet she is also an archetypal trickster. This harmonious melding of attributes in her soul is itself a sign of her God-filled nature, another manifestation of her existence in the space between the physical and supernatural realms.

As a liminal being, Brigid was also able to step over the boundaries of time and geography. As I mentioned earlier, Celtic tradition, with total disregard for what was "realistic" or "possible" according to our modern thinking, honors Brigid as Mary's midwife and Jesus's wet nurse. In another story, Brigid acts as foster mother for Jesus during his parents' escape into Egypt. Still another tale has Brigid traveling forward in time (as well as across space) to the middle of the ninth century (more than three hundred years after her death): as Saint Donatus of Zadar was dying in Florence, Italy, Brigid came to sit at his bedside. He saw a living woman—not a ghost—who talked with him cheerfully, comforting him during his last hours.

Brigid's Mantle

These stories about Brigid tell us as much about the ancient Celts' perception of reality as they do about Brigid. The Celts did not see time as a fixed, linear progression the way we do. They had no problem accepting that a powerfully holy woman like Brigid would be able to slip through time and space according to a logic deeper and more meaningful than any the visible world offers. Brigid moved in Heaven's eternal, ever-present reality.

I admit that one of Brigid's miracles does seem especially fantastical, and I make no claims that this was an actual historical incident. However, though it is one of the least literally possible miracles of Brigid, it may also hold the greatest promise as a signifier of deeper truths. As Lilly said earlier, sometimes story is truer than fact! Jesus understood this, which is why he "hid" his message inside parables. A poem attributed to Columba, a Celtic saint who lived about a century after Brigid, expresses this idea well: "If every poem is a lie, then clothing and food are lies too, as are the whole world and even clayey man." The Celts knew that stories, poems, daily life, and human beings were all containers for a greater Truth.

In any event, Brigid's earliest biographer, a seventh-century Irish cleric named Broccan Cloen, wrote this story about Brigid in the long poem known as "Brocca's Hymn":

Lilly Weichberger & Kenneth McIntosh

On a day of heavy rain she herded
Sheep in the midst of a plain;
She spread her mantle afterwards
Indoors across a sunbeam.

Brigid, born on the threshold between the natural and supernatural realms, could matter-of-factly hang her clothes on a sunbeam. While defying physics, this story promises much in the imaginal realm. It points to another connection between the Pagan solar Goddess and the Christian saint, but even more than that, it lifts the limitations of physical reality beyond ordinary restrictions into the realm of infinite possibility. Do we not all yearn for something far bigger than what our society, family, friends, and business associates say is possible? Don't we have dreams that struggle fiercely to break out of the bars of our limited expectations and run wild into space?

Brigid accomplished far greater things than anyone thought possible—and so can we. Her mantle connects us to something larger, more mysterious—a realm where magic and miracle are simple facts of life. And yet Brigid was also an ordinary, real-life woman, with deep connections to the physical world, especially the world of Nature.

4

Brigid and the World of Nature

Lilly

Celtic spirituality's roots grow deep into the Earth. Pagan pre-Christian Celts perceived the invisible world made visible in Nature. As I explained earlier, the word "pagan" came from an old Latin word that meant, literally, "of the land." The long-ago Celtic tribes felt a profound connection to the land on which they lived, and today, modern

Celtic Pagans create personal relationships with the land and the spirits that inhabit it.

Modern Western society, unfortunately, has become disconnected from the Earth, more so than any other culture at any point in history. In our heated, air-conditioned homes, the turning wheel of the seasons has little effect on us. Our food comes to us in plastic packages on grocery shelves, rather than from the plants and animals that live around us. The cycles of living and growing and dying are no longer part of our everyday lives. In fact, we have become so disconnected from the Earth that we are in danger of destroying ourselves and everything on this planet.

As Kenneth and I discussed at the beginning of this dialogue, Celtic spirituality perceives the Divine as imminent—all around us, all the time. For Celtic Pagans, this means that the Earth—part of the reality around us—is sacred, divine, holy. That belief manifests in an intensely spiritual sense of ecology. We celebrate the seasonal changes as a daily, immediate way to reconnect to the Earth. Moving consciously through the seasons gives us a greater awareness of the Divine within our lives, and it nurtures within us a deep, deep respect for all beings.

One of the fascinating things about Celtic mythology is that it's one of the only mythologies—actually the only one I have found, and I have studied mythology from around the world—that does not have a creation story. The Celts' earliest legends refer to the coming of various groups of people and the conflicts between them, but there is no reference to the moment when the world began.

There's good reason for this. Celtic spirituality perceives creation as something that is constantly happening. It is constantly in motion; there is no beginning, no end to the cycle. The Celts' refusal to see the world and time in terms of linear movement is reflected visually in the twists and turns of their artwork, lines and patterns that have no beginning or end, only points of transformation.

Modern-day Celtic Pagans still see time as a circle that never stops turning. This overarching concept is rooted in the wheel of the year, the cycle of the seasons that brings change and transformation to the land, to plants, to animals, and to human beings. This perspective makes us more consciously aware of Nature.

As a result, we realize that not only human beings are sacred and ensouled, but all beings are; they are all manifestations of the Divine, and therefore they are worthy of our respect and honor. If all of us—Pagan, Christian, Jewish, Muslim, atheist, whatever—could learn to regard all creation as holy, not merely as an inanimate profit source, then maybe we would have a chance of saving the planet, as well as ourselves as a species.

Brigid is a wonderful symbol of this profound sense of ecology. Her very identity is intertwined with the natural world. As the daughter of the Dagda, the Celtic Father God, and Danu, the Mother Goddess, she inherited a strong connection to the entirety of creation.

Some Christians think of God the Father as a powerful, authoritarian figure on a throne, but the Celtic concept of the Father God is quite different. The Dagda does not look down on his creation from some lofty height; he is far too earthy for that. His very being is interwoven with the land and all life. He's also a jovial, joking fellow, who reminds us not to take ourselves and our lives too seriously. When our egos start running the show, he's likely to give us a poke in the ribs or pull a prank, reminding us to lighten up and let go. His personality reminds us that when we have a living relationship with the Earth, we can no longer think of ourselves as the center of the world. It breaks open our egos and makes room in our hearts for compassion and reverence.

The Dagda is connected to the land's fertility, and as his daughter, Brigid too has fertility powers. She is the Goddess of childbirth, and she is also the Goddess of the flocks and herds. When the ancient Celts saw their sheep's and cows' bellies grow big with new life, they knew Brigid had blessed them.

Brigid's mother, Danu, probably the oldest Celtic Deity, gave her daughter a still broader relationship with the natural world. Danu's name is found throughout Celtic lands attached to various rivers (the Danube, for example), hills, mountains, and other land formations, but especially, always, with water. She is the source of life; she is the water that upholds and nurtures the Earth. The word *danu*, meaning "water," is a very ancient one, older even than the Celts; it comes from the Proto-Indo-European language (from which all modern Indo-European languages are descended) that was spoken from around 4500 BCE until 2500 BCE. A thousand or so years later (more than three thousand years ago), when the Rigveda, the Hindu sacred scriptures, was written, it named Danu as the Goddess of the primeval waters. Danu has been around a long, long time!

And Brigid takes after her mother. She too has a deep, nurturing relationship with water, especially with rivers, springs, and wells. Across the British Isles, holy springs and wells bear her name, and in England, the rivers Braint and Brent are named after her.

As Kenneth said, the ancient Celts believed springs and wells were entrances into the Other Realms. This meant that waters had great healing power. Sacred springs were sites of pilgrimage, and people made offerings at them to give thanks for healing, health, and abundance. They tied prayer cloths—clooties—in the branches of the trees around the springs, and they dropped gifts of gold, silver, jewels, and weaponry into the water. (This practice was so common that when the Romans came along, they often auctioned off the rights to a spring because of the wealth that could be dredged from its depths.) Often, as is the case with many Pagan holy sites, the Christian church adopted the ancient wells and springs and built churches there.

Today, both Celtic Pagans and Celtic Christians continue to seek healing from holy springs. The trees surrounding these springs are still covered with offerings: prayers written on slips of paper, images of Deities, and clooties. One of my favorite holy springs is in the churchyard of Saint John the Baptist in Shropshire on the edge of Wales. The water swells up from beneath the roots of an ancient yew tree, which is guessed to be more than sixteen hundred years old, and the spring is reputed to have healing powers, especially for the eyes, which is one of Brigid's special powers. (The Christian Brigid is also said to heal eyes; at one point, she poked out her own eye and then healed it.) This spring was undoubtedly a place where long-ago Celtic Pagans worshipped, which then became the site of a Christian church that absorbed the old beliefs into itself.

The Celtic Pagans considered that trees growing near holy wells were also sacred, and the Goddess Brigid has a deep love for trees. She's especially associated with the oak tree, due to the oaks at Kildare, and the birch tree, whose name comes from the same ancient root word as her name; the birch was the "shining tree," and Brigid was the "shining one." Brigid is often portrayed carrying a wand or branch from a birch tree. Tapping a cow with a birch branch was a Celtic tradition intended to invoke Brigid's fertility so that the cow would calve.

The Pagan Celts believed that all kinds of trees had special powers, but oak, ash, and thorn were the most powerful. Because trees' roots and branches connected earth and sky, they were regarded as doorways between the worlds. They symbolized the balance and harmony that exists within the natural world, and their new leaves each year were reminders of the rebirth that comes after winter's death. Trees were so important to the Celts' thinking that their alphabet (the ogham) was based on trees, as was their calendar.

When the Romans first came to Celtic lands, history says that they cut down many of the sacred trees.

Caesar's reasons for this are unclear; some historians believe it was an act intended to destroy the old culture of Nature-connected faith, replacing it with a more "reasonable" and "civilized" society, while other historians claim that Caesar wanted to remove any places where native military forces might hide.

Then when the Roman Empire converted to Christianity, the Roman Christian church did its best to destroy the old Pagan ways, including a spirituality that was expressed in trees and water. Celtic Christianity found a way to protect them within its shelter. This meant that the old traditions and beliefs could live on beneath the more modern veneer of Christian faith.

Kenneth

I am grateful that Celtic traditions have enriched Christianity. One of the best examples of this is the way the Christian Celts infused their faith with their ancestors' appreciation for the natural world. Saint Ninian, a Celtic Christian who lived during the early 400s, offers us a perfect summary of how the Celts felt about their faith. At about the same time that Patrick was sharing the gospel in Ireland, Ninian was doing the same thing in Scotland. To teach the new converts, he wrote a little catechism, summarizing the most important beliefs of the Christian faith. The second question of that catechism was, "What is the fruit of study?"—and Ninian answers, "To perceive the eternal word of God reflected in every plant and insect, every bird and animal, every man and woman." This is a view of creation that gives equal value to bugs and people! God is woven through all of Creation, said Ninian, and our task is to perceive that reality. Saint Aidan, the first Celt to bring the story of Christ to the Anglo-Saxon people, said something very similar. Like Ninian, he came up with some very basic rules for his followers, things he wanted them to understand about what it meant to follow Jesus. One of them is, "See every person as a child of God, and see everything as a creature of God."

So Lilly's and my perspectives on the Divine immanence within Creation are very close to each other. The world is permeated with God. According to Celtic theology, God is incarnate not only in Christ; the Divine incarnated first in Nature and all the cosmos.

When we look at the stories told about Brigid the Christian saint, we see that the Celts' affinity with Nature and animals did not end with the coming of Christianity. Legend says that Saint Brigid particularly loved and blessed a great oak at Kildare. No one dared harm even a leaf from it, and under its shade she built her cell.

Another legend tells of a group of hunters chasing a wild boar. They'd been after this fierce, tusked creature all day, but he continued to elude them. The hunting party chased the beast right into Brigid's monastery. The hunters were about to come running in after it, spears and all, but Brigid barred their way.

"Stop!" she shouted. "This is holy ground, a place where all can find sanctuary. The boar has come into this holy ground and claimed sanctuary, so you cannot kill it."

"No," the hunters argued, "the boar is an animal. The rule of sanctuary applies only to people."

"Well," Brigid replied, "I'm the abbess and what I say goes. The boar has sanctuary."

Finally, cursing under their breath, the men left. As Brigid turned away from the gate, smiling, one of the monks ran up to her. "This creature is creating holy havoc," he told her. "It's tearing up the place."

So Brigid called the boar to her—and he obeyed. She laid her hands on him and prayed, and he became a docile, loving creature that was a pet at the monastery for the rest of his days.

There are many Brigid stories like this one. Clearly, she was the spiritual older sister of Saint Francis of Assisi, who is considered the patron saint of Nature. Another story, retold from my book *Water from an Ancient Well*, is about the king of Leinster's pet fox.

The king had trained the fox to do tricks, and he loved it very much. One day, though, a workman saw the fox outside the palace and killed it, thinking that it was a wild animal. Passersby saw this deed, seized the man, and took him to the king. The king exploded with fury and grief, then ordered the workman's death.

When Brigid heard of this incident, in the words of her biographer Cogitosus, she "grieved in her inmost heart." She called for her chariot, jumped in, and thundered off toward the king's palace, praying as she went. As the chronicle relates, "The Lord heard Brigid's ceaseless prayers. He told a wild fox to come to her. The fox ran quickly across the plains to Brigid's chariot. It jumped nimbly up into the chariot and sat quietly under her cloak."

So Brigid came to the king and pleaded for the workman's life. As she expected, the king refused, so she produced the fox that had come to her en route to the palace. But the king was uninterested in a surrogate pet: his fox had been trained to do clever and unusual tricks; a wild fox would not delight him the same way. Then, to everyone's astonishment, Brigid gently requested that the wild fox do all the tricks the king required—and it did! Amazed, the king commanded that the workman be let go.

And there is more to the story. The wild fox had a mind of its own and did not want to be the king's pet. In Cogitosus's words: "As Brigid was traveling home the fox weaved through the crowds, outwitted many horsemen and dogs, and fled across the open plains and escaped unharmed to the wild desert places where his den was located."

Stories like these illustrate that same deep ecology that Lilly spoke about. For the Celts, Nature is not something inanimate, there for our convenience. It's not something to buy and sell, throw garbage on, tear up, recklessly mine, and exploit. Instead, it's something to cherish, something with which we can have a loving relationship.

All the Celtic saints, not just Brigid, have stories about their interactions with animals. Saint Kevin, for example, is said to have remained in prayer so long, his hands uplifted, that a blackbird lit on his hand, built a nest there, and then laid an egg. The story goes that Kevin was so full of "patience and love" that he held his hand up until the young bird had hatched and was ready to fly away. What a wonderful symbol of humanity inconveniencing itself for the sake of our fellow creatures!

From a Christian perspective, these stories are also snapshots of the Peaceable Kingdom we believe God wants to call into being. Brigid does not subjugate the fox or the boar, but instead finds a way to achieve peace and harmony. The fox hears the Divine voice just as much as Brigid does. In the end, the fox is still free, and the boar is loved and happy. The Christian Celtic perspective puts Nature and humans on an even level. Both can receive God's voice, and both can reveal Divine reality.

This means that for me, every day is filled with Divine encounters. I was encountering God in every person I met today. As I spoke with them, whether they were rude or pleasant, likable or annoying, I was having a God meeting. And then, as I looked at the falling flakes of snow and the way it clung to the trees' branches, I was also experiencing God. I was seeing God everywhere. God is near, God is here. God is present to us in every person, every tree, ever bird and beast, stone and plant.

An old Celtic prayer expresses this well, describing the way God sends peace to us through Nature.

Deep peace the Earth shall breathe to you,
O weariness, here,
O ache, there!
Deep peace, a soft white dove to you.

Deep peace, a quiet rain to you.
Deep peace, an ebbing wave to you.
Deep peace, the red wind of the east to you.
Deep peace, the grey wind of the west to you.
Deep peace, the dark wind of the north to you.
Deep peace, the blue wind of the south to you.
Deep peace, the pure red of the flame to you.
Deep peace, the pure white of the moon to you.
Deep peace, the pure green of the grass to you.
Deep peace, the pure brown of the soil to you.
Deep peace, the pure silver of the dew to you.
Deep peace, the pure blue of the sky to you.
Deep peace, the pure gold of the sun to you.
Deep peace of the running wave to you.
Deep peace of the flowing air to you.
Deep peace of the quiet Earth to you.
Deep peace of the sleeping stones to you.
Deep peace of the stars to you.
Deep peace of the Son of Peace to you,
Who shines everywhere in this sweet Earth,
Deep, deep peace!

The Celtic Christians took this perspective for granted. Their culture was embedded in the natural world, allowing them to live out their lives with a constant consciousness of the beauty and rhythms of the Earth. Animals and humans and the entire natural world work together, according to the impulses of the Divine that is both within and beyond all creatures. Together, they become the Reign of God, a movement that is gradually advancing in order to eventually restore the entire Earth.

The Celtic saints' interactions with animals were a sign of God's Kingdom overlapping with the here-and-now. Today, Christians often talk as though Heaven and the second-coming of Christ are something that lie ahead, not here, not now—but the Celts had a different way of thinking about the coming-of-God into the world.

As Lilly has explained, pre-Christian Celtic teachings never talked about the beginning of the world—and they didn't talk about the end of the world either. Instead, Pagan Celts had a cyclical version of time. In contrast with that, Western culture, and especially American culture, has focused on the concept of the Apocalypse—a fiery judgment where everything comes to a violent end. That concept has infiltrated even our movies, our pop culture. But the Christian Celts weren't terribly interested in the Apocalypse, and I think their lack of interest was because their ancestors held to that cyclical version of time.

I looked at all the early Celtic sermons I could find and located only three passing references to a final judgment.

When I looked at Anglo-Saxon sermons from the early Middle Ages, however, I found that most—somewhere around 70 percent—talked about an end-of-time judgment and apocalypse. Instead of the Celts' cyclical concept of time, Pagan Anglo-Saxons believed in the *Götterdämmerung*, a final catastrophic battle between gods and giants, with lots of blood, gore, and chaos. The Anglo-Saxons were already obsessed with these end-of-time notions before they converted to Christianity, so when they adopted the new faith, they focused on the biblical stories of a final, violent confrontation with evil. I believe subsequent Western Christianity's emphasis on this violent end—continuing with all the end-time prophecy preachers you see on television today—has its roots back there in Anglo-Saxon culture.

The Celts, however, had a different focus. Brigid and her boar, Kevin holding the blackbird nest until the egg hatches in his hand—these stories and other stories of the Celtic saints were all saying that the Kingdom of God doesn't come violently and dramatically in some far-off day and age. Instead, it's a little seed that keeps growing right now. In the Gospels, Jesus used this image: a Divine Kingdom that grows like a plant, slowly transforming the Earth until humans and animals, plants and soil, water and air are once more in harmony. For the Celts, this gradual journey back to the Garden of Eden was what was meant by the coming of the Reign of God. In Eden, the Christian Celts believed, humans and animals were partners, and this is the *natural* state to which we will be restored. They saw God's plan as a wheel that, as we humans work to make a better world, turns slowly but continuously forward.

This is a deeply hopeful perspective, but it requires an active realignment of our attitudes and actions. It means that as modern-day Celtic Christians we don't look at these stories about Brigid and the other Celtic saints as just interesting tales. Instead, they ask something of us. They require that we look at our lives, take responsibility for all the ways we personally fall short of the Reign of God, and then work to change our own lives and our society.

Lilly

When Kenneth talks about personal responsibility, I couldn't agree more. This is a key concept within Pagan spirituality. We too believe that it is ultimately up to us to bring back balance, to reforge connections between humanity and the rest of Creation. We believe that as we become attuned to the presence of the Divine in Creation, we move toward regaining that place of balance.

Kenneth's story about the boar and the blackbird echoes Pagan legends of human interactions with animals. The Celts, like many other Pagan groups, believed that certain animals were more closely in tune with the Other Realms; the boar and blackbird were two of these creatures. The boar is symbolic of leadership, of forging new paths, regardless of what others may think. He represents the ability to see beneath the surface of things, to see the beauty beyond the rough exterior, to tame primal forces and put them to good use. As for the blackbird, we speak of it as both the bird of the forge and the spirit of inspiration (which means it belongs to the Goddess Brigid!). The blackbird represents that still small voice within us: the muse, the sparks of creativity, our intuition, the presence of the Divine.

When the Goddess Brigid and the Christian Brigid merged to create a bridge between Celtic Paganism and Celtic Christianity, they forged a new path—but Brigid, in both her forms, kept alive the depths and richness of the old traditions. She did not let us lose sight of the ways in which we grow spirituality through our connection with Nature. She continues to remind us that our responsibility to the Earth is part of our spiritual journeys—and that our relationship with Nature is as real and important as our relationship with other human beings.

5

Brigid and Human Relationships

Lilly

Imagine for a moment that you are alive in the Celtic world that existed a thousand years ago. It is mid-winter, when the nights are the longest, and the darkness is deep and cold. You have been out all day tending your sheep, hoping you have enough fodder to get the flock through the winter. You know the darkest and hungriest days of the year are still ahead.

Brigid's Mantle

As you walk through the darkness, you see your cottage ahead, a glimmer of firelight shining warm through the doorway. You smell on the wind the scent of a peat fire and food. You are chilled to your very bones, and so you hurry a little faster.

When you reach the door and go inside, you find a cauldron of stew bubbling over a leaping fire, tended by a beautiful woman with fiery red hair. She welcomes you with a smile and hands you a bowl of food. You settle yourself next to the hearth, and gradually you stop shivering. You know that the warmth of her presence drives the chill from your heart and bones as much as the fire does.

This woman by the fire is Brigid. Her fire brings inspiration and connection with the Divine, but it also offers warmth, comfort, a sense of home. She is the Goddess of the Hearth, the place where human beings come together to find safety, comfort, warmth, and food. Her fire represents the very flame of life that burns at this most intimate nexus of human relationships. From this focal point, Brigid spreads her compassion out into the world.

As I said earlier, Brigid has three aspects. She is the poet and priestess, the smith and patron of the arts, and she is the guardian of hearth and home. As a domestic Goddess, she also functions as a healer and midwife.

She is the Goddess I turn to again and again when I'm helping a client on a healing journey. Brigid works alongside me to create transformation and healing for my client, either through her aspect as healer and nurturer to the wounded soul, or as a midwife who is a catalyst for the birth of a new and stronger part of the individual. (She can also be, as I mentioned earlier, a smith who purifies and shapes us through our experiences in life.)

As the Goddess of the hearth, Brigid fulfills what are traditionally considered women's roles: midwifery, healing, cooking, and tending the hearth and home. The Celts had no problem, however, combining this aspect of Brigid with her role as Mistress of the Forge, where she was often shown wearing a leather apron, tongs in one hand and a sword in the other.

Many Pagan traditions have masculine gods of smithcraft and the forge; Brigid is the only Goddess of the forge I've encountered in my studies, which is a testament to the egalitarian nature of Celtic society. Celtic women were valued and respected not only as mothers, wives, and daughters, but also as warriors, queens, priestesses, and craftswomen.

The Celts' egalitarian culture was clearly reflected in their spirituality. Celtic Paganism (and all Paganism) honors both the male and female aspects of the Divine, the God and Goddess in many different forms. Masculine and feminine aspects of the Divine are seen as equal, and both are necessary. Each has a role, but those roles aren't necessarily based on gender, because the Celts had a fluid perspective on gender roles. Brigid as the Goddess of smithcraft is a perfect example of this.

Brigid offers Pagan women today a role model, demonstrating a healthy and dynamic balance between our roles. As women, we can be mothers and nurturers, while at the same time we demonstrate our power and authority in our careers and other endeavors. Brigid shows us the way.

Kenneth

Like the Goddess Brigid, the Christian Brigid has had a strong influence on gender roles and relations between the sexes. As we've both said already, the ancient Celts were ahead of their time in terms of women's equality and the corresponding importance of a feminine Divine.

The Bible indicates that Jesus and the early Jesus movement also empowered women. However, Hellenistic culture was strongly patriarchal, and as Christianity fell under Imperial ways, it too began to oppress women.

But the earliest Celtic church stayed true both to the beliefs of their Pagan ancestors and the teachings of Jesus. Brigid's life demonstrates this. As much as later biographers may have tried to rewrite the story, the earliest histories make clear that she held a position of authority that was higher than that of most men. Her influence on later Celtic evangelism, monastic life, and ecclesiastic leadership was immense.

What does this say for Christ-followers in the twenty-first century? Sadly, some Christians still deny women's equality. They highlight specific texts within the Bible to support their misogyny, even though the Christian scripture can also be seen as a document of women's liberation. In this divided milieu, the examples of women like Brigid, who had enormous positive influence in the history of the church, are particularly important. Just as the Goddess Brigid is a role model for modern women, so too is the Christian saint.

What's more, female saints like Brigid may help to remind us of God's feminine aspects. This doesn't mean, however, that we think of Brigid as a goddess. Though

Brigid's Mantle

Lilly and I share deep respect for Brigid, this is a place where we differ. While Lilly experiences fulfillment through worshipping the Goddess, I do not worship her as a deity. I respect her as a role model, and I ask her to pray on my behalf, but I do not make my requests to her as a goddess.

Having said that, Christians through the ages have sought for sacred feminine images, such as Mary, Brigid, or the Virgin of Guadalupe, because our traditions have repressed the Divine Feminine, even though she does exist in our scripture and ancient traditions. For example, English Bibles translate one of the Hebrew names for God, *El Shaddai*, as "God Almighty"—but a literal rendering would be "The Many-Breasted One." If we paid more attention to scripture like this, we might have an image of the Almighty Mother suckling the created world, instead of imagining God as an old man with a beard. Likewise, the Hebrew word for the Spirit of God (*Ruach*) is feminine, yet very few churches refer to the Holy Spirit as "she." In the Gospels, Jesus was apparently quite comfortable taking on a feminine role for himself when he said he longed to gather people "as a mother hen gathers her chicks." On another occasion, Jesus compares God to a housewife searching for a lost coin. The language used in the Christian scriptures often equates Jesus with Sophia, the feminine personification of wisdom in the Greek translations of the Hebrew scriptures.

Unfortunately, centuries of Christianity based on Roman philosophy have buried these insights, rendering God as essentially masculine rather than masculine-and-feminine. If many of us are drawn to the idea of a goddess, perhaps it is because the feminine aspects of our Deity have been repressed, hidden from our view.

Swiss psychologist Carl Jung suggested a dual nature to the human soul: the anima (female) and animus (male). As men, Jung taught, we need to have a relationship with the feminine side of their own natures, and as women, we need to affirm and respect the strength of the anima. Jungian writer Robert A. Johnson points out in the book titled *He: Understanding Masculine Psychology*:

> Man has only two alternatives for relationship to his inner woman: either he rejects her and she turns against him in the form of bad moods and undermining seductions, or he accepts her and finds within a companion who walks through life with him giving him warmth and strength.

Maybe the attraction many men feel toward Brigid is because she enables us to reconnect with that feminine aspect within ourselves. This may help explain why veneration for Brigid (and similar female saints) seems to be as strong among men as among women. I recall walking in downtown Los Angeles behind an enormous man with huge rippling muscles, the very picture of masculine power—and the bulging bicep of his left arm was covered completely with an enormous tattoo of the Virgin Mary.

Meanwhile, women, trying to function in a world that often demeans or rejects them, may try to repress their own anima, allowing their animus to become a harsh tyrant rather than a strong supporter. Jungian author M. Esther Harding writes that a woman should seek to find her intrinsic value "through a deeper experience of her own nature which leads her into relation to . . . the feminine principle itself." As Lilly has pointed out, Brigid offers women a role model, someone whose anima and animus work together in healthy harmony. She affirms a woman's strength and authority.

Even deeper than Jungian ideas about anima and animus is a far simpler concept. All of us had mothers. They bore us in their wombs, sustained us at their breasts, offered us sympathy and guidance as we were growing up, and no matter how imperfect or flawed they may have been, never stopped loving us. My mother was taken from me suddenly, before her time to leave (at least that's what I experienced, even if God had another perspective). How many times after that I have wished I could talk to her again, get her advice, gain help from her love and her wisdom! I find comfort, though, imagining Mom as part of the "great cloud of witnesses" in heaven (Hebrews 12:1), cheering me on as she watches from a celestial dimension—and I also take comfort in Brigid, the foster mother of my Gaelic heritage. Brigid comforts the lonely, homesick child that lives inside us all.

Lilly

I agree wholeheartedly with Kenneth's description of Brigid as a strong, loving feminine presence. The Pagan Goddess and the Christian saint are not so different in this respect.

Long ago, when the Roman church supplanted the more holistic and Earth-connected Celtic version of Christianity, it either demonized the pre-Christian Deities or relegated them to myth and fairytales. Brigid, however, was an exception. Her influence was so deep and abiding that it could not be easily stamped out. Instead, she was woven into Christian tradition as the Virgin Mary's midwife. She was often invoked during childbirth to bless the birth and make it swift and safe, and then to bring healing and health to the mother and infant. Christian midwives traditionally "sained" or blessed the child in the name of both Brigid and the Trinity. Alexander Carmichael, who collected traditional Celtic prayers and spells from the people living in the Scottish highlands during the nineteenth century, recorded that "when the woman is in labour, the midwife goes to the door of the house, and standing on the doorstep, softly beseeches Bride to enter, saying 'Bride, Bride, come in! Thy welcome is truly made. Give thou relief to the woman, and give thou the conception to the Trinity.'"

As Ken has mentioned, Celtic Christians also believed that Brigid was the foster mother of the Christ. The story went something like this: One night when Brigid out walking among the oaks of Kildare, she was taken up in a dark blue mantle by two angels. They whisked her away, through time and space, to Bethlehem where the newborn baby Jesus needed her to be his foster mother. Later, when Joseph, Mary, and

Jesus had to flee to Egypt, Brigid aided their escape by appearing as a burning fire between them and the pursuing soldiers.

The transformation of Brigid from Goddess to foster mother of Christ indicates an astonishingly harmonious negotiation between the old and new faiths. The role of foster mother was incredibly important in Celtic tradition. The practice of fostering children among different members of the clan was a way to keep the peace, reinforce kin and clan connections, provide children with training, and share knowledge and skills between different groups. The foster parents' place in the child's life was considered to be sacred, of equal and sometimes greater importance than birth parents'. All this meant that in the Celtic mind, Brigid's role as Christ's foster mother was a powerful one. It was a way to maintain the Goddess Brigid's importance and strength even as she transformed into a Christian saint.

The mention of the mantle in the story is an interesting one. In Celtic stories, a mantle always symbolizes a liminal place of transformation. Adamnan, the biographer of another Celtic saint, Columba of Iona, wrote that before Columba's birth, an angel appeared to his mother with a mantle of marvelous beauty in which were woven the lovely colors of every flower.

This mantle then increased in size until it exceeded the width of the plains. As we've mentioned, Brigid's mantle was also said to be able to increase in size as needed.

Brigid's mantle served to transform liminal space into a place of love, compassion, safety, and healing. Early Celtic Christians believed that her mantle was a "lorica"—a spiritual "breastplate" and a form of mystical protection from all harm. Her mantle was often invoked by the sick, with these words: "Brigid spread thy mantle of protection over me." For modern Celtic Pagans as well, Brigid continues to demonstrate her great compassion for those who are in need.

Kenneth

Along the same lines, Saint Brigid was known for her love of the poor. The saying is that there was never any person who was refused food, clothing, or shelter if they came to Brigid's monastery. I have a prayer card with an old icon of Brigid printed on it. In this image Brigid holds her wheat-straw cross in one hand, and in the other hand she holds a scroll, which bears these words:

> *To care for the poor,*
> *To lighten everyone's burden,*
> *To comfort the suffering.*

I think that triplet nicely summarizes Brigid's role in the world of human relations.

So many of her miracles are related to helping people. Her compassion for others brought about miracles that not only gave people what they needed but also created an abundance that demonstrated God's immense generosity. Her cow could endlessly produce milk, or a flagon of ale could feed a huge host of people, or when she needed mead, honey came out of a stone wall. These miracles are much like Jesus feeding the five thousand with a few loaves and fishes; they are miracles of endless supply and miraculous produce. Like all miracles, they go beyond the events themselves to serve as signifiers, signposts to deep Divine truth. In this case, they show us not only God's abundance but that we too can give—much more than we think we are capable of giving.

Brigid understood that we encounter Christ in "the least of these," his hungry, lonely, or homeless brothers and sisters. (See Matthew 25:31–46.) And Christ still asks his followers to care for others' physical needs. I cannot consider myself his follower in the tradition of Brigid and other Celtic saints if I ignore people who are literally hungry. I may not face-to-face run into a hungry person every day—but the World Health Organization says six million die every year from hunger-related issues. That's the same as the number of deaths from the Holocaust, but this happens every year! Hunger is still the world's biggest problem, and the agony is preventable. Just a small increase of compassion from those of us who live in the developed world could turn that tide.

At the same time we must also be sensitive to other types of hunger in those we encounter daily. Someone once wrote Mother Teresa and said, "I want to come to Calcutta and help serve the poor." Mother Teresa replied, "There are people in need everywhere, find your own Calcutta and serve there." Brigid says the same thing. She's the ultimate embodiment of the impulse to serve, an archetype of charity. She's the Mother Teresa of the Celtic lands, and she inspires me and many others to make a difference by helping others.

She is also the patron saint of beer and mead, something many of my friends of Scot and Irish ancestry can celebrate. We have only one piece of ancient writing that we can say with any certainty may have been composed by Brigid, and it's a prayer that begins, "I would like a great lake of ale for the King of Kings." The prayer ends, "I would like to be watching Heaven's family drinking it through all eternity."

There's a beautiful simplicity about this prayer, a spiritual love that's rooted in the physical world. She's an Irish woman, and she knows what guests like! They like to have the beer horn brought to them, and surely Christ must be the same way. Her prayer expresses her longing to give Christ a gift that has no limits. The prayer also reveals Brigid's understanding that Heaven is a place of close relationships, not only with God but with each other—a family where all share in the gifts we each bring.

Human relationships have always been a vital part of Celtic life, for both Pagan and Christian Celts. Although Celts encouraged each person's uniqueness, they also relied on the community; they lived from womb to grave in close proximity with others in a way that few of us do today. The ancient Celts experienced life as a circle—or a knot, like the intricate designs they drew—of interwoven relationships. Theirs was a friendly universe, where family and clan, Nature, and spiritual forces were all connected endlessly, with no boundary lines between them.

This sense of community transferred easily from the Pagan Celts to their Christian descendants, where it was oftentimes expressed through the church. Although many people in the twenty-first century struggle with what "church" means, I still believe in what the Christian scriptures call the Body of Christ, a living community we rely on for spiritual growth and support. It isn't always easy and it's never perfect—in fact, the challenge of getting along within a spiritual community is sometimes a way God tests us—but I require the company of others who share similar beliefs and practices.

Church can take many forms, however, and today, we may be in the process of finding new ways to live out this ancient concept. My wife and I are part of the Community of Aidan and Hilda, a worldwide network of believers following the waymarks of the Celtic Christian lifestyle. It's a great encouragement to me that I can belong to a wide circle of people that seek to follow Christ with similar Celtic practices. Each member has an anamchara—a soul friend—for personal support and confession, a Celtic practice that was already in place in Brigid's day.

A very old Celtic proverb says, "A person without a soul friend is like someone without a head," indicating how important the Celtic church felt this relationship to be. Without it, a person lacked direction, balance, and vision. In his book *Soul Friendship: Celtic and Desert Insights* (to be released by Anamchara Books), Ray Simpson gives a good explanation of this:

> Anamchara literally means "friend of the soul," and the soul in Celtic thinking, as in biblical language, refers to the total self. It does not refer to a piece of a person, the spiritual bit, as in Greek thinking, which splits the spiritual from the material. Instead, "the soul" refers to the whole person—body, mind, and spirit.
>
> The Anamchara was someone with whom a person could talk through practical matters, reveal hidden intimacies, and break through the barriers of convention and egotism to an eternal unity of soul. Irish soul friendships were graced with affection. Soul friends learned from each other, partaking of secrets so true that that they reached places other friendships could never reach.

When Brigid noticed that a monk in her monastery was lacking the customary company of his anamchara, she asked him, "Where is your soul friend?"

He replied, "He fell ill and died."

Brigid then told him, "Now you must pray and quickly find another anamchara." While her comment may feel a bit cold (uncharacteristic of Brigid), it shows the vital necessity of this arrangement for spiritual life. Perhaps Brigid knew that in the midst of the man's grief for his soul friend, he was all the more in need of spiritual companionship and guidance.

When Brigid said she wanted to give "Heaven's family" a great lake of beer, she was referring to the communion of saints, a network of people that includes anamcharas, family, friends, and the entire worldwide spiritual community, both past and present. After all, if time has no meaning in eternity, then we can believe that Brigid and others are still there, still working actively for the Kingdom of God.

This is a concept that Catholic Christians tend to be more comfortable with than Protestants. Fearing that people would worship the saints instead of God, Protestants discouraged the practice of asking them for help. The Celtic Christians, however, with their nonlinear concept of time, had no trouble appealing to individuals who were strong in the faith—even when they happened to be dead.

According to this very old Christian practice, we pray *to* God *through* the assistance of the saints. We don't *need* to go through the saints—we can speak directly to God—and they never take the place of Christ in our lives. As Christians, we believe Jesus in the only mediator between God and mortals in terms of our redemption (1 Timothy 2:5); nonetheless, we ask human friends to intercede for us all the time, and I consider my relationship with the saints to be much the same.

Most of us as Christians have a living friend who, officially or unofficially, is a "prayer partner." For many years, we may have asked these friends to pray for specific concerns as they arise in our lives. When these individuals die, I can't imagine they would want to stop praying for us as they continue living on a higher plane of existence. In the same way, I cannot believe that Brigid—with a lifelong passion for others and their needs—would cease praying for us. So I can ask Brigid for prayer like I would ask a living prayer partner. I know that her connection with the Divine was deep and strong, and I believe it continues to be.

6

Brigid's Mantle: Connecting the Past to the Present

Kenneth

If you were to visit the Cathedral of Saint Sauveur in Bruges, Belgium, on February first, you'd find inside a glass case a fleecy crimson wool rectangle, a little more than two feet long and about twenty-one inches wide. It's known as Brigid's Mantle.

Of course, relics like this are notoriously difficult to pin down historically. We can't say with absolute certainty, "This scrap of fabric came from a garment owned by a sixth-century saint." Experts have studied the cloth, however, and they've worked with historians to determine a few things.

First, the fabric was dyed with iron oxide and made from wool. A very particular technique was used to create the mantle's shaggy appearance: as the cloth was being woven, tufts of unspun sheep's fleece were intentionally caught into the wool yarn at close, regular intervals. Archeologists have found cloth made in the same way in European Bronze Age graves.

Historians have no concrete evidence to indicate that this type of fleecy fabric was being made in sixth-century Ireland—but by the sixteenth century, references are made by English writers to "Irish shag-rug mantles." Based on other written evidence, we can assume that mantles like this were worn in Ireland at least as early as the twelfth century.

From 1151 to 1224, an Irish abbot named Aéd and his monks were busy writing the Book of Leinster. Aéd was not only an abbot but also the court historian for the King of Leinster (if he had been born seven hundred years earlier, he would have undoubtedly been a Druid!), and he compiled oral history that was well known at the time. Included in his book is a section called "The Taín-bó

Cuailgne" (The Cattle Raid of Cooley), a long story based on pre-Christian events dating back as far as the first century—and within this text are several mentions of "curly-red" kirtles and cloaks.

So yes, it's entirely possible that Brigid would have worn a mantle a made from fabric just like that. But how would it have ended up in Belgium?

There's a quite reasonable historical answer. The earliest reference to the mantle's being in Bruges is 1066, when it was given to the cathedral by Princess Gunhild, the sister of King Harold, the last Anglo Saxon king of England. After her brother died at the Battle of Hastings (where William the Conqueror led the decisive victory that spearheaded the Norman conquest of England), Gunhild fled to the Flemish city of Bruges, in what is today Belgium.

The next question is this: how would an Anglo Saxon princess have ended up with an Irish holy relic? Again, there's a fairly plausible reason, even if it does have a few holes in the story. History has recorded that in 1051, Gunhild's father took his family on a visit to Dermot, the King of Leinster. Since Leinster is only 30 miles from Kildare, it's more than likely the family would have visited what was the most famous holy shrine in Ireland. Who knows, though, how they came to take possession of a piece of a wool cloth that had belonged to Brigid herself! That's the hole in the story.

But whether this small piece of wool is truly Brigid's mantle is not so important. What's more significant is simply the reverence it invoked—and still invokes—even so far from Celtic lands. Something about Brigid is larger than Celtic history and Celtic spirituality; her mantle really does extend a long, long way!

There's something else meaningful about this scrap of wool. Physical objects alleged to be saints' property remind us that flesh-and-blood historical people were at the center of the legends that grew around them. Whether the relic actually belonged to Brigid, it makes a statement: Brigid was a real person who wore a real mantle. She wasn't some hazy, magic being; she was as physical and touchable as that piece of cloth.

Meanwhile, the cloth remains in the cathedral at Bruges. Once a year, on February 1st, the Feast Day of Saint Brigid, it is brought out so visitors can look at it and wonder.

Lilly

February 1st (or sometimes 2nd) is also Imbolc, the half-way point between the winter solstice and the spring equinox. For Celtic Pagans, it's an important day of celebration.

In the Celtic tradition, we celebrate the cycle of the seasons by recognizing eight holidays: the quarters and cross-quarters of the year's wheel, which are the solstices and equinoxes, and the halfway points between them. The Celtic year starts at Samhain (All Saints Day or Halloween), on the evening of October 31st. For the Celts, a new day begins at sunset, not sunrise, not in the light but in the dark. We recognize that the creative act of life begins in darkness, within the womb, rather than with the birth itself, and so, through the winter months, we consider the dark days to be womb time, dream time, the time of creation. Then we come to Yule, which is the rebirth of the sun, the moment when the days begin to get longer and the nights shorter. Even though the sun is reborn at Yuletide, however, it's not very noticeable yet. The nights may be growing shorter, but they're still long and cold! We are still in the depths of winter. Not until Imbolc can we tell that the light is truly returning. Now we know we will make it through the winter and into the springtime and then Midsummer's Day. Darkness will not last forever.

We celebrate Imbolc as the time when the Goddess transitions from her crone and winter aspect into the Maiden of Spring. It's a time of renewal, a time when new life arises out of death, a time that shows us that creation is continual and ongoing. On this day, we honor Brigid's role as protector of hearth and home—of the fires that light our way through the dark times of winter—as well her role as a fertility Goddess. Imbolc, a Gaelic word that refers to sheep pregnancy and lactation, is the time of year when lambs are born. In ancient times, the birth of lambs would bring a ready supply of milk to feed the tribe through the rest of the late winter and spring, until the land could again provide sustenance.

The snowdrop flower is one of the first to appear after winter, in some regions poking up through the snow right about the beginning of February. An old saying is that Brigid walks across the land, strewing snowdrops from her mantle. And then, as spring progresses, she flings out her mantle and turns the world green.

Modern-day Imbolc celebrations remind us that Brigid is alive today, just as she was in long-ago times. Since she is a Goddess of fire, many modern Imbolc traditions involve flame. In Britain, fire festivals with Morris dancers often commemorate her day. Fire dances are a very ancient tradition; a modern addition is poi, the performing art of fire spinning that's been adopted from Maori culture.

Candles are also a traditional part of Imbolc. A young girl is sometimes chosen to be a representative of Brigid by carrying candles or wearing them on her head. My children go to a school where they celebrate Candlemas (the Christian name for Imbolc) by selecting a girl to go from classroom to classroom (wearing a crown of candles), passing out hot cross buns to all the students; she symbolizes the light and life brought back by the Spring Maiden. In my family, we often make candles on Imbolc, enough to get us through the year until the next Imbolc.

Another thing we've done, especially when my kids were little, was to make a Bride's bed. A Bride's bed (sometimes also called a Breed's bed) is a little bed made for Brigid, set by the hearth to welcome her to come in out of the cold for the night. In the morning, the kids would find that Brigid had left them little treats in her bed.

Another tradition I have adapted into my Imbolc celebration is the practice of Brigid's Augury or "Frith." Traditionally the "Frithir"—the seer—would, while fasting, walk three times barefooted deosil (clockwise) around the fire (though without one I use either a candle or lighted cauldron), invoking Brigid in prayer. The Frithir is then led with eyes closed or blindfolded to the threshold of the house. As Kenneth explained earlier, a threshold, neither within nor outside the house but at the same time both and neither, is a liminal place, a place of unlimited possibilities. The Frithir then places her hands on either side of the door jam and, with eyes still closed, asks a question of Brigid. When she opens her eyes, whatever her gaze lights on is considered to be imbued with meaning as the answer to her query. According to Pagan traditions, seeing certain animals or birds means certain things; some animals are lucky, others are unlucky, and still other can indicate some change that is on its way. As with any folk tradition, the symbolic language is vast and complicated.

When I was living in Britain, I often celebrated Imbolc with Druid groups at Avebury, the stone circle that in some ways is more impressive than Stonehenge. A procession of several hundred people would start in the center of the village and then go through the whole circle of stones into the center. Our ceremonies and celebrations took place there, within the ancient stones.

Lately, my Imbolc celebration often involves taking candles with us into the woods for a candle-lighting ceremony. While we light the flames, we focus on the intentions we wish to plant and nurture for the year. I find that Imbolc is a particularly powerful time for starting new projects of any kind, particularly long-term creative work or something you want to be your main focus for the year.

As modern Pagans reclaim ancient traditions and give them new life, we add meaning and spiritual connection to the present, while at the same time we find continuity with our ancestors. You might say Brigid's mantle offers us space between past and present, a liminal realm of possibility. Because of it, I can call on Brigid to be my companion in the here and now, to help me both spiritually and tangibly.

Kenneth

As Lilly has described her relationship to Brigid, I'm reminded of a Buddhist bodhisattva—a being who constantly returns to Earth in order to aid mortals in their spiritual progress. People call on Brigid's aid for many reasons, including help with the tasks of daily life, but her primary role has always been that of instilling faith, giving courage and strength to those who are spiritually struggling.

Brigid's mantle takes on particular significance as we think of her in this role. Earlier, I told the story of Brigid's presence at the birth of Jesus. While Mary slept, Brigid wrapped the baby in her mantle to keep him warm. Then, according to some Celtic traditions, she returned to her own time and land, bringing with her the blessing of Jesus contained within her mantle. When she shook out her mantle, his blessing spread out across Ireland in an ever-widening circle that would eventually reach around the entire world.

This story may be more symbolic than factual, but historically, Brigid, alongside Patrick, was the one who brought Christ to the Celts. Because of this, Christian Celts sometimes call her Mary of the Celts, as well as the Midwife of Mary. In a very real way, Brigid's life helped give birth to Celtic Christianity.

A traditional Celtic prayer, one of those collected by Alexander Carmichael (mentioned earlier by Lilly), expresses the intimate connections the Celtic Christians felt with Brigid:

> *Brigid of the Mantle, encompass us,*
> *Lady of the Lambs, protect us,*
> *Keeper of the Hearth, kindle us.*
> *Beneath your mantle, gather us,*
> *And restore us to memory.*
> *Mothers of our mother,*

foremothers strong.
Guide our hands in yours,
Remind us how to kindle the hearth.
To keep it bright, to preserve the flame.
Your hands upon ours,
Our hands within yours,
To kindle the light,
Both day and night.
The Mantle of Brigid about us,
The Memory of Brigid within us,
The Protection of Brigid keeping us
From harm, from ignorance,
From heartlessness.
This day and night,
From dawn till dark,
From dark till dawn.

This prayer expresses the concept that Brigid spreads her mantle over homes and fields and human hearts. Her mantle also connects night and day, past and present. She is a companion, intimately present in each day's chores, helping us to see the spiritual significance of ordinary things.

A traditional belief was that on Imbolc, Brigid would bless any cloth that was left outside. Within that household this fabric would then be called Brigid's Mantle, a blanket to bring healing and comfort to those who were sick or sad. A Brigid's Mantle of this sort was once a standard part of the Irish midwife's equipment, to wrap around women before, during, and after giving birth.

As we look at all these traditions surrounding Brigid, it's easy to see examples of the way in which Brigid's mantle has enclosed both Pagan and Christian beliefs. In fact the traditions all seem to blend together, so that we can't always tell where the Goddess leaves off and the saint begins—and vice versa.

But despite these real and obvious similarities, I also continue to note the differences between our two belief systems. Even though Pagans believe in an infinite Divine, they see the universe as a web or a matrix—a vast series of connectedness without a center. Reality in the Old Religion is not a web that comes to one central point, like a spider web does. Instead, it's more like Indra's web in Hindu thought. Every point is connected, without a focal point.

But when Brigid—and Patrick, Ninian, Aidan, and all the other Celtic saints—came along, they gave the Celts a new way of looking at the world. Now they saw the universe as a wheel with an axis. The axis was Christ. The wheel cross took on new meaning for them, because the center point—the intersection of horizontal and vertical—now represented Christ, and the circle around the cross symbolized the way in which everything revolves around that axis. As a modern-day Celtic Christian, that is the way I too see reality—not as a web but as a cross, with Jesus at the center.

Lilly

The web is a good analogy for Pagan beliefs. It's one we use often. We speak of spinning the web, by which we mean creating connections and honoring connections between beings. We do perceive that this web has a center—but the center is everywhere. It's wherever you're at. The center is the soul. So our version of the cross has the soul as the center, the point where we connect with the Divine. The arms of the cross represent the elements in balance and harmony around that center—and our souls in balance and harmony with all of creation.

The other symbol we often use to represent reality is the triskelion. It signifies the threefold meaning we see everywhere: in Brigid's three aspects; in Maiden, Mother, and Crone; in earth, sea, and sky; in Creator,

Sustainer, and Destoyer/Transformer. It reveals how all things circle around each other to become a whole. Reality isn't dualistic, black and white, good and bad; it's a dance. I think that's another difference between Kenneth's beliefs and my own: Pagans have a sense of a balance and movement that doesn't rely on Christianity's static either-or.

My own religious background led me from Christianity—my family started out as Methodists—to a community that followed Meher Baba, an Indian spiritual teacher. I was raised within that community, but even as broad and open as that tradition was, I felt a lack of masculine and feminine balance. I longed for a greater focus on both sides of Nature: the dark and the light, creation and destruction, and most of all, the creative interplay between them. For me, I found this balance within Celtic Paganism.

That is another way we look at the triskelion: as a symbol for the creative forces, the deconstructive forces, and the tension between their polarity. That tension is the triskelion's third arm. Positive and negative, creative and destructive: together they give birth again and again and again. So that third arm is more than the sum of the other two combined. It is the Divine Spirit, who constantly cycles through creation, preservation, destruction.

For me, that aspect of Paganism puts perspective on our world. It allows me to honor all the manifestations of Creation and all the ways that humans interact. Good and bad are left behind. Instead of flat black and white, we perceive depth and shades, all the many beautiful hues of the rainbow. This approach isn't as simple and concrete as other ways of looking at life. It doesn't let you put people and events into neat categories. But it leads to a whole other way of connecting that pulls us beyond the boundaries of ourselves

When I speak of Christianity being dualistic, though, I'm speaking of the Christianity that seems most prevalent. I do see a more holistic perspective in Celtic Christianity.

Kenneth

Even in our differences I see similarities. Ancient Christianity had the concept of *perichoresis*—the three-part Circle Dance of the Godhead. The Greek word means literally "go around" plus "make room for, contain, move forward." Jesus was expressing this concept when he prayed "that they may all be one; even as You, Father, are in Me and I in You, that they also may be in Us" (John 17:21 NASB). God is present everywhere, and the Divine Spirit brings unity.

The triskelion flowed from Pagan Celtic faith into Christian Celtic faith without changing its shape at all. On my office door, I have a Columba's Cross (an even-sided cross within a circle) and in the middle is a triskelion, a reminder that God is always three in one. But at the center of the cross is still that single point: Christ. My relationship with Jesus is personal and intimate, the center point of my life, a reality that is with me at every moment.

Lilly

So despite our differences, we can agree that the Divine is right here, right now. In each thing and every person, in every breath of wind, every fall of leaf, every bird's song, every wail of lament, every child's laugh—the Divine is constantly speaking through everything. Every single being, every soul, every atom of creation is singing to us. If we just stop and listen, the Divine voice is right here.

In Celtic Pagan tradition we speak of the "Oran Mor"—the universal song of Creation—and the "Oran Crigh"—our own harmony or dissonance within that song. We strive to bring our soul song into harmony with the song of the universe. Our relationship with our Deities is a way to bring about that harmony.

Here's another point of commonality between Kenneth's beliefs and mine: we both believe that the spiritual journey is about a personal relationship with the Divine. For me, the Gods are the way I can experience this. They allow me to make personal and grasp—at least at some level—something that is so fathomless, so far beyond human comprehension. Having the Deities to connect to gives me just a little handle on that vastness. That personal relationship (and it *is* a relationship, with all the ups and downs that entails) is what sustains me. I talk to them, and they talk back. I listen to them; sometimes I listen better than others. I have been known to praise them and scream at them in the same conversation. For me, this relationship is very real, very personal, very immediate. It means that my church is always the ground I stand on. In Paganism, any space in which you become aware and focus on the Divine is a sacred space. It's a place where Divine light can shine.

Light is the Goddess Brigid's most important attribute. She is a light bringer, in all the many meanings of that word. She allows me to connect in a personal, friendly, intimate way with the Divine Light.

In pre-Christian days, sacred fires burned at Kildare to symbolize Brigid's access to the spiritual realm. Virgins—Druid priestesses whose power and sexuality belonged to no man, only to themselves—tended the fire for more than a thousand years, making sure it never went out. According to tradition, nineteen women had the task of keeping the fire fed each day—but every twentieth day, the Goddess herself tended it.

When Kildare became a Christian monastery, Saint Brigid didn't extinguish the fire. Instead, the task of tending the fires was passed to the nuns of the abbey. These women kept the fire burning, and on the twentieth day, the abbess—Brigid—was said to feed the fire herself.

The ancient tradition continued down through the years. Seven centuries after the Christian Brigid had died, a historian wrote:

> At Kildare many miracles are recorded, amongst which St. Brigid's fire comes first. They call it inextinguishable because the nuns feed it with so much fuel and so carefully that it has never gone out since the time of Brigid. After her death nineteen always remained and when each had tended the fire on their own night, on the twentieth night the last nun put faggots on the fire saying, "Brigid, keep your own

fire, for the night has fallen to you." The fire being so left is always found still burning in the morning.

The fires never went out until the sixteenth century, when King Henry VIII disbanded the monasteries throughout England, Wales, and Ireland. In 1993, however, the Brigidine Sisters relit the flame—and the perpetual flame of Brigid once more burns at Kildare.

That's a meaningful symbol of the way Brigid connects past and present. Time has never extinguished her light. Her mantle doesn't cast a shadow; it casts light. And—despite our differences—her mantle is still bright and wide enough to contain both Pagan and Christian traditions.

Lilly Weichberger & Kenneth McIntosh

Kenneth

Saint Brigid,
you were a woman of peace.
You brought harmony where there was conflict.
You brought light to the darkness.
You brought hope to the downcast.
May the mantle of your peace cover
those who are troubled and anxious,
and may peace be firmly rooted in our hearts
and in our world.
Inspire us to act justly
and to reverence all God has made.
Brigid, you were a voice
for the wounded and the weary.
Strengthen what is weak within us.
Calm us into a quietness that heals and listens.
May we grow each day
into greater wholeness
in mind, body and spirit.

Brigid's Mantle

Lilly

*May Brigid's presence
bring you comfort and peace,
may her flame warm your heart and hearth,
may her bright fires inspire
your thoughts, words, and deeds.
May you be forged by your trials
and her strong hand
into your most perfect self.
May her cool water
heal and sooth your sorrows.
May her mantle protect you from all harm,
and her presence be a light
to guide you through the darkness,
now and always.
Blessed be.*

O Brigid,
spread over my head
your bright mantle
to guard me.

Water from an Ancient Well: Celtic Spirituality for Modern Life

Author: Kenneth McIntosh
Price: $24.95
Paperback
E-book Available
352 pages
ISBN: 978-1-933630-98-4

Discover the world of the ancient Celtic Christians and find practical insights for living in the twenty-first century. Using storytelling, careful research, and personal experience, the author invites you to get to know Brendan and Brigid, Columba and Patrick, as well as Myrddin (better known as Merlin) and other lesser-known figures from the great pageant of Celtic history. These stories both entertain and inspire; rooted in legend and history, they offer us here-and-now hope and insight.

"If you want to run away to paradise for a couple of days, and drink living water from a source unlike any other, read Kenneth McIntosh's deeply satisfying book."
—Leonard Sweet, best-selling author and professor

Earth Afire with God: Celtic Prayers for Ordinary Life
Author: Anamchara Books
Price: $12.95
Paperback
E-book Available
120 pages
ISBN: 978-1-933630-96-0

Here are prayers and blessings that sanctify the simplest of daily activities. They remind us to look for the holiness of the everyday and the real presence of God in Creation. They will illumine your life.

"The folks at Anamchara have done a real favor for all of us who struggle to integrate communion with God into our increasingly busy and complex lives. These short but powerful prayers connect daily routines—washing in the morning, starting the car, seeing a child off to school, or sitting at our computer—with the comforting Divine Presence. This book knocks the dust off ancient treasures--such as selections from *The Carmina Gadelica*—and introduces some lovely new prayers as well."
—Kenneth McIntosh, author of *Water from an Ancient Well: Celtic Spirituality for Modern Life*

Celtic Nature Prayers: Prayers from an Ancient Well

Author: Kenneth McIntosh, compiled by Lucie Stone

Price: $14.95

ISBN: 978-1-62524-263-1

Commune with God in nature using these ancient and modern prayers, with additional text written by Kenneth McIntosh, author of the bestselling *Water from an Ancient Well: Celtic Spirituality for Modern Life*. The Celts found the Divine in every tree and blade of grass, and we too can be refreshed and enriched by this primal love for the Earth. This prayerbook offers a Nature-focused collection based on ancient Celtic prayers, weaving together words of hope, worship, and challenge. Each prayer is an opportunity to connect our personal faith with the Earth we share. As we integrate these prayers into our personal prayer practices, we will gain a new awareness of the urgency of our planet's plight, while we deepen our awareness of its sacredness. The prayers also work well as an opening or closing for gatherings and meetings, to remind those present to turn their hearts to the Earth. Using these Celtic patterns of prayer, we become rooted in an ancient tradition that has always integrated spirituality with an awareness of the Earth. This Celtic form of "green spirituality" creates a desperately needed twenty-first-century pathway to greater spiritual and practical commitment to Nature.

Magic Reversed
Author: Kenneth McIntosh
Price: $14.95
Paperback
E-book Available
133 pages
ISBN: 978-1-62524-240-2

This book can be enjoyed on several levels. It's an action-packed young adult fantasy, brimming with adventure, danger, and romance. Young adult readers will relate to the tension between Finn and Freya that slowly blossoms into something deeper. Fantasy-lovers of all ages will be delighted to encounter characters from Celtic mythology: the wizard Merlin, the Goddess Brigid, and the ravenous walking dead spawned by the Dark Lord's cauldron. At the same time, those who are attracted to Celtic spirituality will find strands of symbolism, like gold threads in an ancient tapestry, meshed unobtrusively with this tale of a young hero's journey to save his world.

Forest Church: A Field Guide to a Spiritual Connection with Nature

Author: Bruce Stanley

Price: $14.95

Paperback

E-book Available

133 pages

ISBN: 978-1-62524-008-8

Brimming with insights and packed with information, this book draws you out, quite literally, into nature to experience a new, well thought through pattern of spiritual practice. Bruce Stanley gives you all the resources you'll need, both practical and theoretical, to get going with a group or on your own.

"I'd rather be in the mountains thinking about God, than in church thinking about the mountains," wrote John Muir.

Many people can describe transcendent moments in nature where they feel deeply connected to something bigger than themselves and Forest Church is a way to explore that connection within community; a new way of being church.

Anamchara Books
Books to Inspire
Your Spiritual Journey

In Celtic Christianity, an *anamchara* is a soul friend, a companion and mentor (often across the miles and the years) on the spiritual journey. Soul friendship entails a commitment to both accept and challenge, to reach across all divisions in a search for the wisdom and truth at the heart of our lives.

At Anamchara Books, we are committed to creating a community of soul friends by publishing books that lead us into deeper relationships with God, the Earth, and each other. These books connect us with the great mystics of the past, as well as with more modern spiritual thinkers. They are designed to build bridges, shaping an inclusive spirituality where we all can grow.

To find out more about Anamchara Books and order our books, visit **www.AnamcharaBooks.com**.

Anamchara Books
Vestal, New York 13850
www.AnamcharaBooks.com

www.ingramcontent.com/pod-product-compliance
Lightning Source LLC
Chambersburg PA
CBHW060527080526
44586CB00012B/652